Animal Fun Facts

Over 750 Fun Facts about Animals Guaranteed to Blow Your Mind

Volume 1

MENTAL BOMB PUBLISHING

INTRODUCTION

This fascinating book contains over 750 fun facts about 50 of the most amazing animals in the world that are guaranteed to blow your mind!

Did you know that Polar bear fur appears white, but it is translucent, allowing sunlight to reach their black skin, which helps in retaining heat?

Did you know that a cat's nose print is as unique as a human's fingerprint, making it a reliable form of identification?

Did you know that Dolphins have a unique way of sleeping? They rest one hemisphere of their brain at a time, allowing them to stay partially conscious and continue breathing while sleeping.

The animal kingdom is extraordinary, astonishing, and full of fascinating surprises!

So, what are you waiting for? Let's dive into the incredible and fascinating realm of creatures big and small, from the depths of the ocean to the heart of dense jungles.

Prepare to learn astonishing facts about the remarkable behaviors and incredible adaptations that make the animal kingdom a tapestry of awe and wonder.

Enjoy!

MENTAL BOMB
Our goal is to entertain and to blow your mind!

Visit us online at MentalBomb.com
Home for the best illusions, riddles, games, and fun facts!

Follow

Facebook: Mental-Bomb-
Instagram: mental_bomb_
Pinterest: Mental_Bomb
Twitter: MentalBomb_

CONTENTS

1. ALLIGATORS

Alligators are large, semi-aquatic reptiles belonging to the Alligatoridae family. They are closely related to crocodiles and are native to the southeastern United States and parts of China. Alligators are characterized by their robust, broad bodies, muscular tails, and powerful jaws filled with sharp teeth. They have armored skin covered in thick scales, providing protection and buoyancy in water.

In the wild, alligators inhabit freshwater habitats such as swamps, marshes, and rivers. They are excellent swimmers and can stay submerged for long periods, using their eyes and nostrils positioned on the top of their heads to keep a watchful eye on their surroundings while partially submerged. Alligators are carnivorous predators, feeding primarily on fish, amphibians, birds, and small mammals. They are known for their stealthy hunting techniques, relying on patience and ambush to catch their prey.

Despite their intimidating appearance, alligators play a crucial role in their ecosystems. As top predators, they help regulate prey populations, and their burrows provide shelter for various other species during droughts or extreme weather conditions. However, they face threats due to habitat loss, pollution, and human interactions, and conservation efforts are essential to ensure their survival in the wild. In some areas, alligators have become a symbol of local pride and are protected by law to preserve their natural populations and maintain ecological balance.

o Alligators have been around for over 37 million years, making them living dinosaurs!

o Alligators are excellent swimmers and can reach speeds of up to 20 mph (32 km/h) in the water.

o Their jaws are incredibly powerful, capable of exerting 3,700 pounds per square inch (psi) of bite force – that's stronger than most animals!

o   Alligators are masters of the "death roll" – a move used to subdue and tear apart their prey.

o   Female alligators are devoted moms – they build nests and fiercely protect their eggs until they hatch.

o   You can tell the difference between alligators and crocodiles by their snouts – alligators have a U-shaped snout, while crocodiles have a V-shaped snout.

o   Alligators are cold-blooded, relying on the sun to warm themselves up.

o   They can hold their breath underwater for up to an hour – a great skill for stealthy hunting!

o   Alligators create special "gator holes" that provide vital habitats for other animals during droughts.

o   Alligators communicate using growls, hisses, and bellows, especially during the mating season.

o   They have a unique valve in their throats called the glottis, which lets them breathe even when their mouths are submerged.

o   Alligators can detect vibrations in the water from far away, helping them sense nearby movement.

o   The average lifespan of an alligator in the wild is around 35 to 50 years, but they can live much longer in captivity.

o   Alligators can regenerate their teeth throughout their lives, so they never run out of teeth for chomping!

o   Ever wondered how alligators survive the cold? They enter a state of dormancy called brumation during colder months – like reptilian hibernation!

2. BALD EAGLES

The Bald Eagle (Haliaeetus leucocephalus) is a majestic bird of prey and the national bird of the United States. It is well-known for its striking appearance, with a white head and tail contrasting against a dark brown body. Adult Bald Eagles have a wingspan that can reach up to 7 feet (2.1 meters) and can weigh between 8 to 14 pounds (3.6 to 6.3 kilograms). These impressive birds are known for their powerful flight and keen eyesight, which allows them to spot prey from great distances.

Bald Eagles are mainly found in North America, primarily near large bodies of open water such as lakes, rivers, and coastal areas. They prefer habitats with abundant fish, which make up a significant portion of their diet. While fish are their primary food source, they are opportunistic hunters and will also feed on birds, small mammals, and carrion.

These birds are known for their impressive hunting skills and are often seen soaring high in the sky or perched on trees near the water's edge, patiently waiting for an opportunity to dive and catch their prey. The Bald Eagle's impressive appearance and symbolism of freedom have made it an iconic symbol of the United States and a beloved species that is protected under strict conservation laws to ensure its survival in the wild.

o   The Bald Eagle is not actually bald. Its name comes from the old English word "balde," which means white-headed.

o   They have remarkable eyesight and can spot a fish from up to 2 miles (3.2 kilometers) away!

o   Bald Eagles can reach speeds of up to 30 to 35 mph (48 to 56 km/h) when flying.

o   These birds are skilled hunters and can catch fish with their talons while flying at full speed.

o   Bald Eagles are powerful swimmers and can use their wings like paddles to help them swim.

o   Bald Eagles often steal food from other birds, like Ospreys, by harassing them until they drop their catch.

o   They build large nests, called "aeries," made of sticks in tall trees near bodies of water.

o   Bald Eagles can have wingspans of up to 7 feet (2.1 meters).

o   These birds are known for their courtship rituals, which involve aerial displays and acrobatic flights with their mates.

o   Bald Eagles are known for their distinctive calls, which include high-pitched whistles and throaty cackling sounds.

o   They are highly territorial and will defend their nesting territories fiercely.

o   The Bald Eagle became the national emblem of the United States in 1782.

o   These birds are not only skilled hunters but also excellent scavengers, often feeding on carrion.

o   The Bald Eagle's call is not what you might expect! Instead of a majestic, powerful roar, its call sounds more like a high-pitched, weak "peep," which is surprising given its grand appearance.

3. BEARS

Bears are large, powerful mammals belonging to the family Ursidae. They are known for their robust bodies, stocky build, and distinctive snouts. There are several species of bears found around the world, including the polar bear, brown bear, black bear, and giant panda, each with its unique characteristics and habitats. Bears have sharp claws and powerful jaws, making them formidable predators, although their diet can vary significantly depending on the species and their environment.

Bears are widely distributed across various continents, with different species inhabiting diverse ecosystems, ranging from polar ice caps to dense forests and mountainous regions. They are highly adaptable animals, and some species, such as the brown bear, are known to cover vast territories in search of food and mates. Bears are omnivores, meaning they consume a mixed diet of plant matter, such as berries and grasses, and animal food, including fish, insects, and occasionally larger mammals.

These magnificent creatures play essential roles in their ecosystems as both predators and scavengers. They help regulate prey populations and aid in nutrient cycling by consuming and dispersing seeds through their feces. Conservation efforts are crucial to protect these iconic animals and preserve their critical role in maintaining ecological balance.

o   Bears are excellent swimmers and are known to swim long distances in search of food or to reach new habitats.

o   Despite their large size, bears can run surprisingly fast, with some species reaching speeds of up to 30 mph (48 km/h).

o   Polar bears are the largest land carnivores and have been known to weigh up to 1,500 pounds (680 kilograms)!

o   Bears have an exceptional sense of smell, which allows them to detect food from miles away and is crucial for their survival.

o   Some bear species, like the brown bear and black bear, are excellent climbers and can easily ascend trees to escape predators or reach food.

o   Bears are generally solitary animals, except for mothers with cubs or during the breeding season.

o   The fur color of black bears can vary widely, ranging from black, brown, cinnamon, or even a bluish hue.

o   Bears are incredibly intelligent animals and have demonstrated problem-solving skills and memory capabilities in various studies.

o   During hibernation, a bear's heart rate, body temperature, and metabolic rate drop significantly, allowing them to survive for months without food or water.

o   Bears have a unique mating behavior called "delayed implantation," where the fertilized egg does not immediately attach to the uterus, allowing the female to delay giving birth until the timing is right.

o   While bears are known to be strong and powerful, they can also be quite agile and have been observed performing impressive acrobatics.

o   The front paws of bears have five toes, while the rear paws have four, and their claws are strong and sharp, aiding in climbing, digging, and catching prey.

o   Bears play an important ecological role as "ecosystem engineers," meaning their activities, such as digging, help create habitats for other species.

o   The giant panda's diet is almost exclusively bamboo, and they can eat up to 40 pounds (18 kilograms) of it daily!

o   Bears are skilled foragers and have a varied diet, which may include fish, berries, insects, small mammals, carrion, and more.

4. BEES

Bees are flying insects known for their essential role in pollination and honey production. They belong to the family Apidae and are closely related to wasps and ants. Bees have distinct characteristics, such as a pair of wings, six legs, and specialized body structures for collecting nectar and pollen. They are social insects, with many species forming colonies that consist of a queen, worker bees, and drones.

Pollination is one of the most crucial contributions of bees to the ecosystem. As bees collect nectar from flowers to make honey, they inadvertently transfer pollen from one flower to another, facilitating the fertilization of plants. This process is vital for the reproduction of many flowering plants and the production of fruits and seeds. Without bees' pollination services, global food production and biodiversity would suffer significantly.

Honeybees are the most well-known bee species for their honey-making capabilities. They store honey in wax combs within their hives and use it as food during times when nectar is scarce. The surplus honey produced by honeybees is harvested by beekeepers for human consumption. Beyond honey production and pollination, bees also produce other products like beeswax and royal jelly, which are used in various industries and traditional medicine. Conservation efforts are essential to protect bees and ensure their critical role in maintaining ecosystems and food security.

o   Bees are the only insects in the world that produce food that humans can eat – honey!

o   Honeybees communicate through "dances." They perform the famous "waggle dance" to indicate the direction and distance of a food source to other hive members.

- Bees have two stomachs – one for eating and the other for storing nectar to take back to the hive.

- There are over 20,000 known species of bees, with various colors, sizes, and behaviors.

- Bees have five eyes – three small ones on top of their head and two large compound eyes on the sides.

- Some bee species, like bumblebees, can fly at high altitudes and even at sub-zero temperatures.

- Bees are incredibly hard workers. A single honeybee may visit up to 2,000 flowers in a day!

- They are experts at geometry. When building honeycomb cells, bees make them hexagonal, the most efficient shape for storing honey and raising their brood.

- The male bees in a colony are called "drones." Their primary role is to mate with a queen from another colony.

- The queen bee can lay up to 2,000 eggs in a single day, ensuring the colony's population.

- Bees are essential pollinators for many fruits, vegetables, and flowers, contributing significantly to global food production.

- The famous "killer bee" is a hybrid of African and European honeybees, known for their aggressive behavior when threatened.

- Bees have been around for millions of years, with fossil records dating back around 100 million years.

- Bees have excellent memories and can recognize specific flower shapes and scents, making them efficient foragers.

- Beeswax, produced by worker bees, is used to build honeycomb cells and has various applications in cosmetics, candles, and even art.

5. BUTTERFLIES

Butterflies are beautiful and graceful insects belonging to the order Lepidoptera. They are known for their vibrant colors, delicate wings, and unique life cycle. Butterflies have four distinct stages of metamorphosis: egg, larva (caterpillar), pupa (chrysalis), and adult (butterfly). During the caterpillar stage, they voraciously eat plant matter to store energy for their transformation into a pupa. Once they emerge as butterflies, they embark on their brief but remarkable adult life, primarily focused on reproduction and pollination.

These insects play a crucial role in the ecosystem as pollinators. As butterflies feed on nectar from flowers, they inadvertently transfer pollen from one flower to another, aiding in the fertilization of plants. This process is essential for plant reproduction and the production of fruits and seeds. Butterflies are particularly attracted to brightly colored flowers and those with sweet scents. Their role as pollinators makes them valuable contributors to biodiversity and food production.

Butterflies are found on every continent except Antarctica, with a vast diversity of species inhabiting different habitats, from tropical rainforests to arid deserts. Their wing patterns and colors vary significantly, providing them with a range of adaptations for camouflage, mimicry, and mate recognition. Their stunning beauty and captivating flight have made butterflies symbols of transformation, renewal, and freedom in many cultures around the world.

o   Butterflies taste with their feet! They use special sensors on their feet to detect the chemical composition of the surfaces they land on.

o   Butterflies have four wings, which are covered in tiny scales that give them their vibrant colors and patterns.

- The wings of butterflies beat between 5 to 20 times per second during flight, depending on the species.

- Some butterflies, like the Monarch butterfly, undertake long-distance migrations, traveling thousands of miles each year.

- Butterflies can see ultraviolet light, allowing them to detect patterns on flowers that are invisible to humans.

- Unlike most insects, butterflies do not have a mouth to chew. Instead, they use a long, straw-like proboscis to sip nectar from flowers.

- The lifespan of butterflies varies significantly among species, ranging from a few days to several months.

- Some butterflies, like the Glasswing butterfly, have transparent wings that make them nearly invisible against certain backgrounds.

- Caterpillars have a voracious appetite and can eat several times their body weight in plant matter each day.

- Butterflies hibernate during the winter. They enter a state of rest called "diapause" to survive the cold months.

- Some species of butterflies, like the Blue Morpho butterfly, are iridescent, meaning their wings shimmer and change colors in the light.

- Butterflies communicate with each other through chemical signals released by special glands on their wings and bodies.

- The painted lady butterfly holds the record for the longest recorded butterfly migration, traveling up to 9,000 miles (14,500 kilometers) round trip.

- Butterflies have specialized adaptations to avoid predators, such as eyespots on their wings to scare away potential threats.

- The world's smallest butterfly, the Western Pygmy Blue, has a wingspan of only 0.5 to 0.75 inches (1.3 to 1.9 centimeters).

6. CATS

Cats are domesticated carnivorous mammals belonging to the Felidae family. They have been companions to humans for thousands of years, valued for their hunting skills and ability to control pests. Cats are known for their grace, agility, and independence. They come in various breeds, each with unique physical traits and personalities, from the sleek and athletic Siamese to the fluffy and gentle Maine Coon.

Cats are highly adaptable animals, capable of thriving in a variety of environments. They are skilled hunters and have keen senses, including excellent night vision and acute hearing. Cats communicate using body language, vocalizations, and purring, which can indicate their contentment and comfort. They are known for their grooming habits, constantly cleaning their fur to keep it in pristine condition.

As pets, cats form strong bonds with their owners, providing companionship and affection. They can be playful and social, enjoying interactive playtime and cuddling with their human family members. Cats have distinct personalities, and each one can have unique preferences and behaviors. Their ability to understand human emotions and show empathy further enhances their role as beloved family members and treasured companions.

- o   Cats have a unique grooming pattern. They lick themselves to keep clean and remove loose fur, and their rough tongues work like natural brushes.

- o   Cats have a flexible backbone that allows them to twist and turn their bodies, making them exceptional acrobats and climbers.

- o   A group of cats is called a "clowder" or a "clutter."

o Cats have a special reflective layer behind their retinas called the tapetum lucidum, which enhances their night vision.

o The world's oldest known pet cat was found in a 9,500-year-old grave on the island of Cyprus.

o A cat's purr is not just a sign of contentment; it can also be a way to self-heal and relieve stress.

o Cats have an extraordinary sense of balance, allowing them to land on their feet after falling from heights.

o The average cat sleeps for about 12 to 16 hours a day.

o Cats communicate with humans and other cats using a variety of vocalizations, including meows, purrs, chirps, and trills.

o The record for the world's longest domestic cat measured over 3 feet (about 1 meter) from nose to tail.

o Cats' whiskers are highly sensitive and can help them navigate and detect changes in their environment.

o A cat's nose print is as unique as a human's fingerprint, making it a reliable form of identification.

o The richest cat in history was named Blackie, inheriting £15 million (equivalent to around $28 million) from his owner, a British antiques dealer.

o The "catnip" plant contains a compound called nepetalactone that acts as a stimulant for cats, causing temporary euphoria and excitement.

o Cats can rotate their ears independently, allowing them to pinpoint the direction of sounds with exceptional precision.

7. CHEETAHS

Cheetahs (Acinonyx jubatus) are magnificent and agile big cats known for their incredible speed and striking appearance. They are native to Africa and some parts of Iran and are part of the Felidae family. Cheetahs have a slender, athletic build, characterized by their distinctive black tear stripes running from the eyes to the mouth and their spotted golden-yellow coats. These markings help reduce glare and provide camouflage in their natural grassland habitats.

Cheetahs are the fastest land animals, capable of reaching speeds of up to 60 to 70 miles per hour (97 to 113 kilometers per hour) in short bursts. They have specialized adaptations for speed, such as long and muscular tails for balance and a lightweight body structure. Unlike other big cats, cheetahs have non-retractable claws, which provide better traction for running at high speeds. Their speed is essential for catching prey, as they mainly hunt small to medium-sized ungulates like gazelles and impalas.

Despite their incredible athleticism, cheetahs face various challenges in the wild, including habitat loss, human-wildlife conflicts, and a reduced genetic diversity that affects their ability to adapt to environmental changes. They are listed as vulnerable by the International Union for Conservation of Nature (IUCN), and conservation efforts are crucial to ensure the survival of these magnificent cats in their native habitats. Cheetahs are truly a symbol of grace and speed, capturing the hearts of many and embodying the wild beauty of the African savannas.

o   Cheetahs are the fastest land animals, capable of accelerating from 0 to 60 miles per hour (97 kilometers per hour) in just a few seconds.

o   Unlike other big cats, cheetahs cannot roar. Instead, they communicate through various vocalizations, such as chirping, growling, and purring.

- Cheetahs have excellent eyesight, allowing them to spot potential prey from far distances.

- They have black "tear stripes" running from the eyes to the mouth, which help reduce glare and improve their vision during hunts.

- Cheetahs have unique, semi-retractable claws that provide better traction for running at high speeds.

- Cheetahs are daytime hunters, preferring to hunt during early morning or late afternoon when temperatures are lower.

- Unlike other big cats that rely on brute strength to bring down prey, cheetahs use their speed to chase and trip their prey.

- Cheetahs are solitary animals, except for mothers with cubs. They typically hunt and live alone.

- They have a specialized respiratory system with enlarged nasal passages and lungs, which helps them take in more oxygen during high-speed chases.

- Cheetah cubs have a unique appearance, with long, fluffy tufts of hair on their backs known as a "mantle." The mantle helps camouflage them in tall grass.

- Cheetahs have a high reproductive rate compared to other big cats. They can have litters of up to six cubs, although the average litter size is three to four cubs.

- Cheetahs are diurnal animals, meaning they are most active during the day and rest at night.

- A cheetah's spots are solid black, and they cover the entire body, including the belly.

- Despite their incredible speed, cheetahs have a low success rate in hunts, with estimates suggesting that they are successful only about 30% of the time.

8. CHIMPANZEES

Chimpanzees (Pan troglodytes) are highly intelligent and social primates belonging to the Hominidae family. They are native to the tropical forests of Central and West Africa. Chimpanzees share about 98% of their DNA with humans, making them our closest living relatives. They have a robust build, with long arms and opposable thumbs, which allow them to grasp and manipulate objects effectively.

Chimpanzees live in complex social groups known as communities, with each community led by a dominant male known as the alpha male. Within these communities, individuals form strong bonds, display various social behaviors, and communicate through vocalizations, body language, and facial expressions. They are known for their use of tools, such as using sticks to extract insects from termite mounds or cracking nuts with stones. This tool usage showcases their cognitive abilities and problem-solving skills.

Chimpanzees are omnivores, consuming a wide range of foods, including fruits, leaves, insects, and occasionally small mammals. They are adaptable and can thrive in various habitats, from dense rainforests to savannas. Conservation efforts are crucial to protect these incredible primates and ensure their survival in the wild, preserving their vital role in the ecosystems they inhabit.

o   Chimpanzees are skilled climbers and spend much of their time in trees, swinging from branch to branch using their long arms.

o   They have excellent memory and can remember the location of fruit trees and other valuable resources for extended periods.

o   Chimpanzees use a variety of facial expressions, vocalizations, and gestures to communicate with each other, expressing emotions such as joy, anger, and fear.

o They have been observed using leaves as "sponges" to soak up water and then drinking from them.

o Chimpanzees are known for their playfulness and engage in various games, such as chasing and wrestling with each other.

o They are one of the few animals capable of recognizing themselves in a mirror, indicating a level of self-awareness.

o Chimpanzees have distinct personalities, and their behaviors can vary from one individual to another within the same community.

o They are highly adaptable and have been known to modify tools for different purposes, such as using sticks to fish for termites or using stones to crack nuts.

o Chimpanzees are skilled problem solvers and can devise creative solutions to obtain food or achieve their goals.

o They are one of the few animal species that engage in warfare, with communities occasionally engaging in violent conflicts with neighboring groups.

o Female chimpanzees have been observed using tools more frequently than males, highlighting their resourcefulness in gathering food.

o Chimpanzees form strong bonds with their family members and engage in grooming to build and maintain social relationships.

o They can live up to 50 years or more in captivity, but their lifespan in the wild is typically shorter due to various environmental challenges.

o Chimpanzees exhibit altruistic behaviors, such as consoling distressed individuals or helping others in need.

o Chimpanzees have a unique way of walking on two legs, known as bipedalism, which they use for short distances, such as when carrying objects or food.

9. CROCODILES

Crocodiles are large, reptilian predators belonging to the Crocodylidae family. They have been around for millions of years and are often referred to as "living fossils" due to their ancient lineage and relatively unchanged appearance. Crocodiles are semi-aquatic creatures, spending much of their time in or near water. They have long, powerful tails, webbed feet, and specialized salt glands that allow them to survive in both freshwater and saltwater environments.

These apex predators have a strong jaw filled with sharp teeth, and their bite force is one of the most powerful in the animal kingdom, capable of exerting tremendous pressure. Crocodiles are opportunistic hunters, preying on a variety of animals, such as fish, birds, mammals, and other reptiles. They are known for their ambush hunting technique, where they wait patiently underwater for unsuspecting prey to approach before striking with lightning speed.

Crocodiles play a vital role in their ecosystems as top predators, helping to regulate the populations of their prey species. They are found in various regions worldwide, primarily in tropical and subtropical areas. Despite their fearsome reputation, crocodiles are important and fascinating creatures with unique adaptations that have allowed them to thrive for millions of years.

o   Crocodiles are ancient creatures, dating back over 200 million years to the Mesozoic Era, during the time of the dinosaurs.

o   They have a unique way of thermoregulation called "gaping." By opening their mouths, crocodiles release heat and cool themselves down.

o   Crocodiles have the strongest bite force of any animal, with some species capable of exerting over 3,700 pounds per square inch (psi) of pressure.

- These reptiles can go without food for weeks or even months due to their slow metabolism.

- Unlike most reptiles, crocodiles are caring parents. Females guard their nests and help transport hatchlings to the water.

- Crocodiles have a transparent third eyelid, called a "nictitating membrane," which protects their eyes underwater.

- They are efficient swimmers, using their tails to propel themselves at speeds of up to 20 to 25 mph (32 to 40 km/h) in short bursts.

- Crocodiles have a lifespan of up to 70-100 years, with some individuals living even longer in captivity.

- These reptiles have specialized salt glands located on their tongues, allowing them to excrete excess salt and tolerate saltwater habitats.

- Some species of crocodiles, like the saltwater crocodile, can travel thousands of miles during migration.

- Crocodiles have a symbiotic relationship with certain birds, such as the Egyptian plover, which clean their teeth and feed on parasites inside their mouths.

- Crocodiles can leap out of the water to catch prey at astonishing heights, sometimes exceeding their entire body length.

- They can regulate their body temperature through basking in the sun or cooling off in the water, depending on their environment.

- Crocodiles can survive in various environments, from freshwater rivers and swamps to coastal and even brackish waters.

- Crocodiles have an extraordinary ability called "galloping." When running on land, they can lift their bodies off the ground and move all four legs in unison, creating a gait that resembles galloping.

10. DOGS

Dogs, also known as Canis lupus familiaris, are domesticated mammals and one of humanity's most beloved companions. They are descendants of wolves and have been living alongside humans for thousands of years. Dogs come in a wide variety of breeds, each with distinct appearances, temperaments, and abilities, reflecting the diverse roles they play in human society.

Dogs are highly social animals, forming strong bonds with their human families and other animals. They are known for their loyalty, affection, and ability to understand and respond to human emotions. As pack animals, dogs thrive in a structured environment and often look to their human owners as their pack leaders. Their keen sense of smell and hearing makes them excellent hunters and guardians, and they have been employed in various working roles, including herding, search and rescue, therapy, and police work.

As pets, dogs provide companionship, comfort, and unconditional love to their human families. They are also known for their playful and energetic nature, bringing joy and happiness to the lives of those they touch. Dogs require regular exercise, mental stimulation, and proper care to lead happy and healthy lives. Their presence in our homes and hearts has earned them the nickname "man's best friend," a testament to the special bond between humans and these incredible creatures.

o   Dogs have an incredible sense of smell, with some breeds capable of detecting scents up to 100,000 times better than humans.

o   The Basenji is a breed of dog that does not bark. Instead, it makes a unique sound called a "yodel" or "barroo."

o   Dogs have a special reflective layer behind their retinas called the tapetum lucidum, which enhances their night vision.

o Dachshunds were originally bred to hunt badgers in their burrows, and their name translates to "badger dog" in German.

o The world's smallest dog breed is the Chihuahua, and the largest is the Saint Bernard.

o Dogs have a special muscle called the "levator anguli oculi medialis," which allows them to give humans the "puppy eyes" look.

o The Australian Cattle Dog holds the Guinness World Record for the longest living dog, reaching 29 years and 5 months old.

o Dogs have a unique nose print, much like a human's fingerprint, making them identifiable.

o Greyhounds are the fastest dog breed and can reach speeds of up to 45 miles per hour (72 kilometers per hour).

o Dogs have a remarkable ability to understand human emotions and can sense when their owners are happy, sad, or scared.

o The term "dog days of summer" originates from the ancient belief that the hottest days of the year coincide with the rising of the star Sirius, also known as the Dog Star.

o The average dog can learn up to 165 words, gestures, and signals, with some highly trained dogs capable of understanding even more.

o Dogs dream, and their brain activity during REM sleep suggests that they may be dreaming about past experiences or activities.

o The Saluki, an ancient breed of dog, is considered one of the oldest domesticated dog breeds, dating back over 7,000 years.

o Dogs are known for their exceptional hearing, capable of detecting sounds at four times the distance that humans can hear.

11. DOLPHINS

Dolphins are highly intelligent and social marine mammals belonging to the family Delphinidae. They are known for their playful behavior, sleek bodies, and remarkable communication skills. Dolphins have a streamlined shape, with a curved dorsal fin and a characteristic beak-like snout. They are well-adapted to life in the water, possessing powerful tails that enable them to swim at high speeds and jump gracefully above the surface.

These charismatic creatures are found in oceans and seas worldwide, inhabiting a variety of environments, from coastal areas to deep ocean waters. They live in tight-knit social groups known as pods, where they display complex communication and cooperative behaviors. Dolphins communicate through a combination of clicks, whistles, and body language, and their intricate vocalizations are believed to convey messages and help maintain social bonds within the pod.

Dolphins are carnivorous predators, feeding on a diverse diet that includes fish, squid, and small marine animals. They have a sophisticated echolocation system, emitting clicks and listening for the echoes to locate and identify prey, demonstrating their remarkable hunting abilities. These captivating marine mammals are admired for their intelligence, agility, and unique adaptations, making them a subject of fascination and admiration for humans and researchers alike.

o   Dolphins are not fish; they are mammals. They breathe air through blowholes located on the top of their heads.

o   Some species of dolphins can swim at speeds of up to 25 miles per hour (40 kilometers per hour).

o   Dolphins are highly social animals and live in tight-knit groups called pods, which can consist of a few individuals to hundreds.

o   Bottlenose dolphins, one of the most well-known dolphin species, can recognize themselves in mirrors, indicating self-awareness.

o   Dolphins use echolocation to navigate and find food. They emit clicks and listen for the echoes to detect objects in their surroundings.

o   A dolphin's skin is sensitive to touch, and they enjoy interacting with each other and humans through gentle touching.

o   Dolphins have a remarkable memory and can remember individual dolphins they have encountered before.

o   Some dolphins display cooperative hunting behavior, where they work together to corral schools of fish for easier capture.

o   Dolphins are excellent problem solvers and have been observed using tools, such as sponges, to protect their noses while foraging on the sea floor.

o   Dolphins are known for their curiosity and may approach boats and swimmers to investigate and play.

o   The largest dolphin species is the Orca, also known as the killer whale, which can grow up to 32 feet (10 meters) in length.

o   Dolphins are known to show compassion and help injured or distressed individuals, both within their pod and with other species, including humans.

o   Dolphins have a specialized "melon" in their foreheads, which helps them focus sound waves during echolocation.

o   Some dolphins exhibit bioluminescence, where they produce their own light through special bacteria on their bodies.

o   Dolphins have a unique way of sleeping. They rest one hemisphere of their brain at a time, allowing them to stay partially conscious and continue breathing while sleeping.

12. ELEPHANTS

Elephants are magnificent and intelligent mammals belonging to the family Elephantidae. They are known for their large size, long trunks, and tusks. There are two main species of elephants: the African elephant (Loxodonta africana and Loxodonta cyclotis) and the Asian elephant (Elephas maximus). Elephants have a social and complex family structure, living in tight-knit herds led by a matriarch, often the oldest and wisest female.

Their trunks are one of the most distinctive features of elephants, serving as a multipurpose tool. They use their trunks for drinking, bathing, breathing, grasping objects, and even communicating through touch and sound. Elephants are herbivores, consuming vast amounts of vegetation daily, including grasses, fruits, leaves, and bark.

Elephants play a crucial role in their ecosystems. They are known as ecosystem engineers, shaping their environments through their feeding habits and movements. They create water holes and clear paths through dense vegetation, benefiting other animal species and helping to maintain the balance of their habitats. Conservation efforts are essential to protect these majestic animals and ensure their survival in the wild for generations to come.

o   Elephants are the largest land animals on Earth, with African elephants reaching heights of up to 13 feet (4 meters) at the shoulder and weighing as much as 14,000 pounds (6,350 kilograms).

o   Elephants have the longest pregnancy of any land mammal, lasting approximately 22 months.

o   Newborn elephants, called calves, can stand and walk within a few hours after birth.

o   Elephants are excellent swimmers and can use their trunks as snorkels while swimming.

o   They communicate using a wide range of vocalizations, including trumpeting, rumbling, and roaring, as well as through body language and infrasound (low-frequency vibrations).

o   Elephants display strong emotional bonds within their social groups and are known to show empathy and compassion towards other members of their herd.

o   African elephants have large ears shaped like the African continent, while Asian elephants have smaller, rounded ears.

o   Elephants are herbivores and can consume up to 300 pounds (136 kilograms) of food in a single day.

o   They use their trunks to gather food, drink water, and dust themselves to protect against insects.

o   Elephants have a unique way of cooling themselves down. They use their trunks to spray water or mud on their bodies, which then evaporates and cools them off.

o   Asian elephants have one "finger" at the tip of their trunks, while African elephants have two.

o   Elephants show a strong sense of self-awareness, as demonstrated in mirror self-recognition tests.

o   They have complex social structures and live in multigenerational family groups led by a matriarch.

o   Elephants can communicate with each other over long distances through infrasound, which can travel up to several miles.

o   The trunk of an elephant contains more than 100,000 muscles, making it a highly versatile and dexterous appendage.

o   Elephants form deep emotional connections and have been known to mourn the loss of deceased family members, showing grief and sadness.

13. ELEPHANT SEALS

Elephant seals are large and remarkable marine mammals known for their size and distinct appearance. They belong to the family Phocidae and are divided into two main species: the northern elephant seal (Mirounga angustirostris) and the southern elephant seal (Mirounga leonina). These seals are named for the trunk-like proboscis that adult males develop on their snouts during the breeding season. While females and young males lack this feature, adult males use their inflatable nose to produce loud roars and assert dominance during territorial battles.

Elephant seals are true champions of the ocean, spending much of their lives at sea and navigating the depths with incredible diving abilities. They are known to dive as deep as 5,000 feet (1,500 meters) and remain submerged for extended periods, sometimes staying underwater for over an hour. Their remarkable adaptations include a large volume of blood and oxygen storage, allowing them to endure such deep and prolonged dives.

During the breeding season, elephant seals gather in colonies on remote beaches and islands. Dominant males, known as bulls, compete for the right to mate with a group of females, forming harems. These breeding battles involve vocalizations, body displays, and fierce confrontations, with the strongest bull prevailing as the harem's leader. Elephant seals are truly extraordinary creatures, captivating the attention of researchers and nature enthusiasts alike with their size, behavior, and unique features that make them some of the most intriguing marine mammals on Earth.

o   Elephant seals are the largest pinnipeds, with adult males weighing up to 8,800 pounds (4,000 kilograms) and females weighing up to 2,200 pounds (1,000 kilograms).

o   They can grow to be about 13 to 16 feet (4 to 5 meters) in length.

o   The "elephant" in their name comes from the large, inflatable proboscis-like nose that adult males develop during the breeding season.

o   Elephant seals can hold their breath and dive for impressive durations, with some reaching depths of around 5,000 feet (1,500 meters) and staying underwater for up to two hours.

o   Unlike many other seals, elephant seals are known to migrate vast distances, sometimes traveling thousands of miles in search of food.

o   These seals are excellent swimmers and can reach speeds of up to 15 miles per hour (24 kilometers per hour) in the water.

o   Elephant seals are mostly solitary creatures outside of the breeding season, but they form massive colonies during the mating season.

o   The male elephant seals engage in fierce battles during the breeding season to establish dominance and gain access to mating opportunities with females.

o   The breeding season for northern elephant seals typically occurs between December and March, while southern elephant seals breed between June and December.

o   Elephant seals have a unique method of fasting during the breeding season, relying on their extensive blubber reserves for nourishment.

o   Female elephant seals give birth to a single pup after a gestation period of about 9 to 12 months.

o   Pups are born with dark fur and weigh around 70 pounds (32 kilograms) at birth.

o   Elephant seals have been known to make vocalizations underwater, producing sounds that can be heard by other seals over long distances.

o   Their blubber layer helps them stay warm and insulates them from cold ocean waters.

o   Elephant seals have sensitive whiskers that aid in detecting prey while foraging in the dark depths.

14. FLAMINGOS

Flamingos are iconic and distinctive birds known for their vibrant pink plumage and long, slender legs. They belong to the family Phoenicopteridae and are found in various parts of the world, including Africa, Asia, the Americas, and Europe. Flamingos are highly social birds and often form large flocks, creating breathtaking displays of pink hues when gathered together.

Their unique pink coloration is a result of the pigments in the algae and small crustaceans they consume, which get deposited in their feathers. Flamingos use their specialized bills to filter-feed in shallow waters, where they tilt their heads upside down to trap food in their bristle-like tongue.

Flamingos are highly adaptable and can thrive in a range of habitats, including salt pans, lagoons, and estuaries. They are excellent waders and are capable of standing on one leg for long periods, which conserves body heat and helps them remain stable in muddy waters. These elegant birds are not only admired for their stunning appearance but also for their graceful and synchronized movements when in flight or during group activities, making them a symbol of beauty and grace in the avian world.

o   Flamingos get their pink coloration from the carotenoid pigments found in the food they eat, such as algae and small crustaceans.

o   The more carotenoids they consume, the deeper and more vibrant their pink color becomes.

o   Flamingos are not born with their pink color; baby flamingos are gray or white and gradually turn pink as they mature.

o   They have a unique way of feeding called "filter feeding." They use their specialized bills to filter tiny food particles from the water.

o   Flamingos often feed with their heads upside down in the water to maximize their efficiency in capturing food.

o   They have a backward-bending knee joint that allows them to stand on one leg for extended periods without much effort.

o   Flamingos are highly social birds and live in large colonies, sometimes comprising thousands of individuals.

o   They communicate with each other through various vocalizations, including honks, grunts, and "fanfare" calls.

o   Flamingos are strong fliers and can reach speeds of up to 35 miles per hour (56 kilometers per hour) when in flight.

o   They are excellent swimmers and use their webbed feet to paddle through the water.

o   Flamingos use their wings as a display during courtship rituals, raising them to show off their bright colors.

o   When they fly, flamingos often form large, V-shaped formations, like those of migratory birds.

o   Flamingos are monogamous during the breeding season, and some species perform synchronized dance displays as part of their courtship rituals.

o   They build nests out of mud, sticks, and feathers, often creating cone-shaped mounds to protect their eggs from flooding.

o   Flamingos have a lifespan of about 20 to 30 years in the wild, although some individuals in captivity can live even longer.

o   The collective noun for a group of flamingos is a "flamboyance."

15. FOXES

Foxes are small to medium-sized members of the Canidae family, which also includes wolves and domestic dogs. They are found throughout various regions worldwide, with species such as the red fox (Vulpes vulpes) being among the most widely distributed. Foxes are highly adaptable and can thrive in a range of habitats, from forests and grasslands to urban areas.

These clever and agile animals have distinctive features, including pointed ears, a bushy tail, and a slender body. Their fur color can vary significantly depending on the species, ranging from reddish-brown to gray and even black. Foxes have excellent senses, including sharp hearing and a keen sense of smell, which aids them in locating prey and detecting potential dangers.

Foxes are omnivorous, meaning they eat both plant and animal matter. Their diet includes small mammals, birds, insects, fruits, and even scavenged food from human settlements. They are solitary creatures for most of the year, only forming temporary social groups during the breeding season. Foxes are renowned for their intelligence, agility, and ability to adapt to changing environments, making them one of the most successful and fascinating wild canines in the world.

o   There are about 37 species of foxes, found in various regions around the world.

o   The red fox is the most widely distributed and adaptable species of fox, found in diverse habitats from forests to urban areas.

o   Foxes have excellent senses, including hearing sounds as quiet as a mouse squeak from 100 feet away.

o   Some fox species, such as the Arctic fox, can change the color of their fur from brown to white during the winter to blend in with their surroundings.

o   Foxes are skilled hunters and can pounce and leap high in the air to catch prey like mice and birds.

o   They are also opportunistic scavengers and will eat fruits, vegetables, and human food leftovers.

o   Foxes use their bushy tails to help with balance, communication, and keeping warm during cold nights.

o   They have retractable claws like domestic cats, allowing them to climb trees and dig burrows.

o   Foxes are mostly solitary, but they do form small family groups during the breeding season to raise their young.

o   Arctic foxes have thick fur and a specialized blood vessel system in their paws to help them withstand freezing temperatures.

o   The fennec fox, native to the Sahara Desert, has large ears that act like radiators, releasing excess body heat and helping it stay cool in the scorching desert environment.

o   Foxes have a wide range of vocalizations, including barks, screams, and howls, used for communication, and establishing territory.

o   Foxes are notorious for their cunning and have been featured in folklore and mythology as clever tricksters.

o   Some species of foxes, like the kit fox, can go their entire lives without drinking water, obtaining moisture from their food instead.

o   Foxes have a unique hunting technique known as "mousing," where they use their keen hearing to locate prey beneath the snow or ground before pouncing.

16. GIRAFFES

Giraffes are majestic and unique creatures known for their towering height and distinctive long necks. They belong to the family Giraffidae and are native to the savannas and grasslands of Africa. Giraffes are the tallest living terrestrial animals, with adult males (bulls) reaching heights of up to 18 feet (5.5 meters) and females (cows) slightly shorter. Their long necks, which can be as long as 7 feet (2.1 meters), allow them to reach vegetation high above the ground that is inaccessible to other herbivores.

These gentle giants are herbivores, primarily feeding on leaves, flowers, and fruits from acacia trees and other shrubs. Their unique feeding behavior involves using their long, prehensile tongues to grasp and strip leaves from tree branches. Giraffes have a specialized cardiovascular system to cope with their height, which prevents blood from rushing to their heads when they lower them to drink water or reach the ground to eat.

Giraffes are highly social animals and often live in loose groups known as herds. Their communication involves various vocalizations, including low moans, hisses, and flute-like sounds. They also use body language, such as necking (sparring) between males, to establish dominance and access to mates. With their gentle demeanor and extraordinary appearance, giraffes continue to captivate the imagination of people worldwide, making them one of the most beloved and iconic animals in the African savanna.

o   Giraffes are the tallest land animals, with their long necks making up about half of their height.

o   Adult giraffes can reach heights of up to 18 feet (5.5 meters) and weigh between 1,800 and 4,300 pounds (800 to 1,950 kilograms).

o   Despite their towering height, giraffes have only seven neck vertebrae, the same number as most mammals, including humans.

o   Their long necks and legs allow them to browse for food at heights that other herbivores cannot reach.

o   Giraffes have distinctive spotted coats, and no two individuals have the same pattern.

o   They have long, prehensile tongues, which can be up to 45 centimeters (18 inches) long, to grasp and strip leaves from tree branches.

o   Giraffes are ruminants, meaning they have a four-chambered stomach to aid in digesting their plant-based diet.

o   Despite their impressive height, giraffes can run at speeds of up to 35 miles per hour (56 kilometers per hour).

o   They are non-territorial animals and often live in loose herds, consisting of females and their young.

o   Giraffes are surprisingly agile and can use their legs to deliver powerful kicks to defend themselves against predators.

o   When giraffes are born, they drop approximately 6 feet (1.8 meters) to the ground, helping them take their first breath and encouraging them to become active quickly.

o   Male giraffes, called bulls, engage in "necking" battles, where they use their long necks to swing their heads at each other in displays of dominance.

o   Giraffes have a unique cardiovascular system with a large heart to pump blood all the way up their long necks to their brains.

o   Giraffes are surprisingly silent animals and communicate mainly through body language and some vocalizations.

o   They have a symbiotic relationship with oxpecker birds, which feed on ticks and other parasites found on their bodies, providing a form of mutual benefit.

o   Despite their towering size, giraffes are surprisingly gentle creatures and are a symbol of grace and beauty in the animal kingdom.

17. GORILLAS

Gorillas are one of the largest and most powerful primates, belonging to the family Hominidae. They are native to the forests of Central Africa and are closely related to humans, sharing approximately 98% of their DNA with humans. Gorillas are highly intelligent and social animals, living in close-knit family groups led by a dominant silverback male. Silverbacks get their name from the distinctive silver hair that develops on their backs as they mature.

Gorillas are herbivores, primarily feeding on a vegetarian diet of leaves, fruits, shoots, and stems. They have a unique body structure, with strong arms and hands that allow them to knuckle-walk on the ground and climb trees. Despite their enormous size, gorillas are known for their gentle nature and are generally non-aggressive unless provoked or threatened.

Conservation efforts are essential to protect these magnificent creatures and their natural habitats. Gorillas are a symbol of conservation and a flagship species for the preservation of the rich biodiversity found in African rainforests.

o   Gorillas are the largest living primates, with adult males (silverbacks) weighing up to 400 pounds (180 kilograms) or more.

o   There are two species of gorillas: the eastern gorilla (Gorilla beringei) and the western gorilla (Gorilla gorilla). Each species has two subspecies.

o   Gorillas have longer arms than legs, making them excellent climbers and knuckle-walkers on the ground.

o   They are primarily herbivores, consuming a diet of leaves, fruits, bark, and vegetation.

o   Silverbacks get their name from the silver-grey hair that develops on their backs as they mature.

o   Gorillas communicate using a variety of vocalizations, body postures, and facial expressions to convey emotions and maintain group cohesion.

o   Despite their size and strength, gorillas are generally peaceful and non-aggressive animals. They prefer to resolve conflicts through displays and vocalizations rather than physical confrontations.

o   Gorillas build nests to sleep in each night, constructing them from leaves and branches in trees or on the ground.

o   A group of gorillas is called a "troop" or "band," and it typically consists of several adult females, their offspring, and a dominant silverback male.

o   Gorillas share a remarkably close genetic relationship with humans, with DNA similarities of around 98%.

o   They have opposable thumbs, which allow them to manipulate objects and use tools.

o   Gorillas have been observed using sticks as tools to extract termites from their mounds for food.

o   A gorilla's life span is around 35 to 50 years in the wild, and they can live even longer in captivity.

o   Gorillas are highly intelligent animals and have displayed problem-solving abilities and cognitive skills in various studies.

o   They are essential for the ecosystem as they play a crucial role in seed dispersal, helping maintain forest biodiversity.

o   Gorillas are listed as endangered or critically endangered, primarily due to habitat loss, poaching, and diseases. Conservation efforts are critical to protect these magnificent creatures and their habitats.

18. HIPPOPOTAMUSES

Hippopotamuses, commonly known as hippos, are large and semi-aquatic mammals found in sub-Saharan Africa. They are among the most massive land animals and are known for their massive size, barrel-shaped bodies, and enormous mouths filled with large teeth. Hippos are primarily herbivores, grazing on grasses and other vegetation near water bodies. Despite their size and seemingly slow movements, hippos are surprisingly agile and can run at impressive speeds on land and are formidable swimmers.

Hippos spend much of their time in the water to keep cool and protect their sensitive skin from the sun. They are well adapted to aquatic life, with their eyes, ears, and nostrils located at the top of their heads, allowing them to see, hear, and breathe while most of their bodies are submerged. Hippos are also known for their vocalizations, which include grunts, roars, and honks, used for communication and establishing territory.

These fascinating animals are known for their aggressive and territorial nature, particularly during the breeding season when male hippos engage in fierce battles to establish dominance. Despite their intimidating demeanor, hippos are herbivorous and rarely pose a threat to humans unless they feel threatened or provoked. However, they are considered one of the most dangerous animals in Africa and are responsible for more human fatalities than any other large mammal in the region.

o   The name "hippopotamus" comes from the ancient Greek words "hippos" (horse) and "potamos" (river), meaning "river horse."

o   Hippos are more closely related to whales and dolphins than to other land mammals.

o   Hippos are excellent swimmers and can hold their breath for up to five minutes underwater.

o   They secrete a reddish, oily substance from their skin, which gives them a unique appearance and acts as a natural sunscreen.

o   Despite their large size, hippos can run at speeds of up to 20 miles per hour (32 kilometers per hour) on land.

o   Hippos are highly territorial and use their large jaws and tusks to defend their territory and establish dominance.

o   They have incredibly powerful jaws, with large canines and incisors that can grow up to 20 inches (50 centimeters) long.

o   Hippos are mostly nocturnal, spending their days resting in water to stay cool and becoming more active at night.

o   They communicate with each other using a series of vocalizations, including grunts, snorts, and wheezes.

o   Hippos are social animals and can be found in groups called "pods" or "bloats," which can consist of up to 30 individuals.

o   Despite their massive size, hippos are herbivores and primarily feed on grasses, fruit, and aquatic plants.

o   The closest living relative of the hippopotamus is the pygmy hippo, a much smaller and less aggressive species found in West Africa.

o   Hippos have an intricate system of scent glands that they use to mark their territory and communicate with other hippos.

o   Baby hippos, called calves, are born underwater and must swim to the surface for their first breath.

o   Hippos have an excellent sense of smell and hearing but rely more on their exceptional sense of touch and vibrations to navigate in murky waters.

o   While hippos are known for their aggressive behavior, they are also social animals and can form close bonds with other members of their pod.

o   The hippo is one of the most dangerous animals in Africa and causes more human fatalities than other mammals in the region.

19. HORSES

Horses are majestic and versatile mammals known for their strong build, speed, and long history of domestication by humans. Belonging to the Equus genus, horses are part of the Equidae family, which also includes zebras and donkeys. They are native to various regions worldwide, including North America, Europe, Asia, and Africa. Horses have been essential companions to humans throughout history, serving in transportation, agriculture, warfare, and sports.

Horses are herbivores, primarily grazing on grass and other vegetation. They have long legs, hooves, and a single solid hoof on each foot, making them swift runners. Their manes, forelocks, and tails are characteristic features that differ between horse breeds and can vary in color and length. Horses come in various sizes, with ponies being smaller and horses being taller.

These intelligent and social animals form strong bonds with other horses and can communicate through body language and vocalizations. Domesticated horses have been selectively bred for specific traits, leading to the development of numerous horse breeds, each with unique characteristics suited to different purposes, such as racing, show jumping, dressage, or pleasure riding. Horses continue to be admired for their beauty, athleticism, and the special connection they share with humans as steadfast companions and partners in various activities.

o   Horses have an excellent memory and can remember people and places for years.

o   The average horse's heart weighs around 10 pounds (4.5 kilograms) and can pump about 10 gallons (38 liters) of blood per minute.

o   Horses have a 360-degree panoramic vision, allowing them to see almost all around them without turning their heads.

- A horse's teeth can reveal its approximate age. As they age, their teeth change in size and shape.

- The fastest recorded speed of a horse was achieved by the Thoroughbred racehorse, Winning Brew, at 43.97 miles per hour (70.76 kilometers per hour).

- A horse's height is measured in "hands," with one hand equal to four inches (10.16 centimeters).

- Horses are social animals and form strong bonds with their herdmates, often displaying grooming behaviors as a way of showing affection.

- The term "horsepower" was coined by James Watt, the inventor of the steam engine, to compare the power of his engines to that of horses.

- Horses have a unique digestive system that relies on fermentation in the hindgut to break down fibrous plant material.

- A horse's hooves grow continuously, and they need regular trimming and farrier care to maintain proper hoof health.

- Horses can sleep both standing up and lying down, thanks to a "stay apparatus" in their legs that allows them to lock their joints.

- The oldest recorded horse lived to be 62 years old, named Old Billy, an English barge horse born in 1760.

- Horses have a strong flight response and can react quickly to perceived threats, often referred to as a "spook."

- The smallest horse breed is the Falabella, which stands about 17 to 34 inches (43 to 86 centimeters) tall at the withers.

- Horses communicate with each other through various vocalizations, including neighs, whinnies, and snorts.

- The horse's sense of smell is highly developed and plays a crucial role in detecting danger and finding food and water.

- Horses can express a wide range of emotions through their facial expressions, including happiness, fear, and curiosity.

20. JAGUARS

Jaguars are magnificent and elusive big cats known for their striking appearance and powerful hunting abilities. They are native to the Americas and are found primarily in dense rainforests, swamps, and grasslands from the southern United States to Argentina. Jaguars have a muscular build, with a distinctive golden-yellow coat covered in black rosettes (spots in the shape of roses) that act as camouflage in their forested habitats.

As skilled predators, jaguars are opportunistic hunters, preying on a wide variety of animals, including deer, peccaries, monkeys, fish, and even large reptiles. They are solitary animals, preferring to hunt and live alone except during mating season and when raising their young. Jaguars are stealthy and powerful, using their exceptional climbing and swimming abilities to ambush their prey from trees or water sources.

Despite their strength and prowess, jaguars are currently listed as "near threatened" on the International Union for Conservation of Nature (IUCN) Red List. They face significant threats from habitat loss, poaching, and conflict with humans. Conservation efforts are vital to protect these iconic and important apex predators and preserve the ecosystems they inhabit in the Americas.

o   Jaguars are the third-largest big cats in the world, after tigers and lions, with males being larger than females.

o   They have incredibly strong jaws and sharp teeth, capable of delivering a powerful bite that can crush the skulls of their prey.

o   Unlike other big cats, jaguars prefer to kill their prey by delivering a single fatal bite to the back of the neck.

- Jaguars are excellent swimmers and are known for their ability to hunt in water, making them unique among big cats.

- The scientific name of the jaguar is Panthera onca.

- Jaguars are solitary animals, except during the breeding season and when mothers are raising their cubs.

- They are known for their impressive climbing abilities and can easily scale trees to ambush prey from above.

- Jaguars have a distinctive coat pattern with rosettes (rose-shaped spots) that are larger and more spaced out than those of leopards.

- The black coloration of some jaguars is called "melanism," and these individuals are often referred to as "black panthers."

- Jaguars have a powerful territorial instinct and use scent markings to establish their range.

- Their name comes from the Tupi-Guarani word "yaguara," which means "beast that kills with one leap."

- Jaguars have a unique preference for hunting in the early morning and evening, known as crepuscular behavior.

- They have a keen sense of hearing and use it to locate prey in dense vegetation or under the water.

- Jaguars can carry prey that is much larger than themselves, such as deer or peccaries, up into trees to avoid scavengers.

- Jaguar cubs are born blind and depend on their mother for care and protection for the first few months of their lives.

- Jaguars are highly adaptable and can be found in a variety of habitats, including rainforests, grasslands, and swamps, throughout their range in the Americas.

21. KANGAROOS

Kangaroos are iconic marsupials native to Australia. They belong to the family Macropodidae, which also includes wallabies and wallaroos. Kangaroos are known for their powerful hind legs, large tails, and distinctive hopping locomotion, which allows them to cover vast distances with remarkable speed and efficiency. These fascinating creatures are well adapted to their arid and varied Australian habitats, including grasslands, woodlands, and deserts.

One of the most notable features of kangaroos is their unique reproductive system. Female kangaroos, known as "does" or "flyers," have a pouch on their belly where they carry and nurse their underdeveloped joeys (baby kangaroos). The joeys continue their development inside the pouch for several months after birth, receiving nourishment and protection from their mother.

Kangaroos are herbivores, primarily feeding on grasses and other vegetation. Their specialized digestive system allows them to extract the maximum nutrition from their fibrous diet. They are also able to go extended periods without water, making them well-adapted to Australia's sometimes harsh and dry climate. With their distinctive appearance, unique reproductive methods, and remarkable hopping abilities, kangaroos continue to be celebrated as one of Australia's most beloved and emblematic animals.

o   Kangaroos are only found naturally in Australia and New Guinea.

o   There are four main species of kangaroos: the red kangaroo, eastern grey kangaroo, western grey kangaroo, and the antilopine kangaroo.

o   A group of kangaroos is called a "mob" or a "troop."

o   Kangaroos are marsupials, meaning females give birth to relatively undeveloped young and carry them in a pouch.

o   Newborn kangaroos, called joeys, are about the size of a lima bean and continue to develop inside their mother's pouch.

o   A female kangaroo can delay giving birth if environmental conditions are harsh, such as during droughts.

o   Kangaroos are excellent jumpers and can cover distances of up to 25 feet (7.6 meters) in a single leap.

o   They are the largest marsupials in the world, with some species of male red kangaroos reaching heights of over 6 feet (1.8 meters) and weighing up to 200 pounds (90 kilograms).

o   Kangaroos have a unique form of locomotion called "pentapedal movement," where they use both hind legs and their tail as a tripod while grazing or moving slowly.

o   To escape from predators, kangaroos can reach speeds of up to 40 miles per hour (64 kilometers per hour).

o   Male kangaroos often engage in "boxing" matches to establish dominance or to compete for mates.

o   Kangaroos have a specialized stomach with four compartments to efficiently digest their fibrous plant-based diet.

o   The kangaroo is featured on the Australian coat of arms, symbolizing the country's unique wildlife.

o   Some kangaroo species are known for their distinctive vocalizations, which include growls, clicks, and grunts.

o   Kangaroos have adapted to hot and dry conditions and are capable of conserving water by producing concentrated urine and limiting sweating.

22. KOALAS

Koalas are adorable and iconic marsupials native to Australia. Belonging to the family Phascolarctidae, they are closely related to wombats. Koalas are famous for their teddy bear-like appearance, with round faces, fluffy ears, and large, expressive eyes. They have a distinctive silver-grey coat with white patches on their chest and are well adapted to their eucalyptus-dominated habitats.

These arboreal creatures spend most of their lives in eucalyptus trees, where they feed on the leaves of various eucalyptus species. Eucalyptus leaves are tough and fibrous, but koalas have specialized digestive systems that allow them to break down these leaves and extract the necessary nutrients. Koalas obtain most of their water from these leaves and rarely drink from other sources.

Koalas are marsupials, and like other marsupials, females have a pouch where they carry and nurse their underdeveloped joeys (baby koalas). After birth, the joey climbs into the mother's pouch to continue its development for several months. Once it is too big for the pouch, it will ride on its mother's back until it becomes more independent.

o   Koalas are not bears; they are marsupials. Their closest living relatives are wombats.

o   Koalas are native to Australia and are found in the eastern and southeastern parts of the country.

o   They have a unique adaptation to their eucalyptus diet, with a specialized digestive system that detoxifies the leaves' chemicals.

o   Koalas have five clawed fingers on their front paws and two opposable thumbs, which help them grip and climb trees easily.

o Their scientific name is "Phascolarctos cinereus," which means "ash-grey pouched bear."

o Koalas have excellent senses of smell and hearing, which help them detect predators and locate suitable eucalyptus leaves.

o They are mostly nocturnal animals, being more active during the night and resting during the day to conserve energy.

o Koalas can sleep for up to 18 to 20 hours a day to support their low-energy diet.

o The name "koala" is believed to have originated from an Aboriginal word meaning "no drink" because they get most of their water from eucalyptus leaves.

o Baby koalas are called joeys, and after birth, they crawl into their mother's pouch to continue developing.

o Koalas communicate through vocalizations, with males often bellowing to establish their territory during the breeding season.

o Despite their gentle appearance, koalas have sharp claws and can deliver a powerful bite if they feel threatened.

o Koalas have a specialized immune system to tolerate the toxic chemicals present in eucalyptus leaves.

o They have a slow metabolism, which helps them conserve energy from their low-nutrient diet.

o Koalas are solitary animals and are generally not social except during mating season or when raising offspring.

o Each koala has a unique nose print, like a human fingerprint, which helps researchers identify and track individuals in the wild.

23. LEOPARDS

Leopards are powerful and stealthy big cats belonging to the genus Panthera, which also includes lions, tigers, and jaguars. They are widely distributed across Africa and parts of Asia, from savannas and grasslands to forests and mountains. Leopards are known for their stunning coat, characterized by golden-yellow fur with dark rosettes (spots in the shape of roses) that provide excellent camouflage in their diverse habitats.

These solitary and elusive predators are highly adaptable and can thrive in various environments. They are primarily nocturnal, hunting at night to surprise their prey, which includes a wide range of animals such as deer, antelopes, monkeys, and small mammals. Leopards are also exceptional climbers and are known for carrying their prey up into trees to protect it from scavengers and to consume it at leisure.

Leopards are expert stealth hunters, relying on their keen senses of sight and hearing to locate and stalk their prey. They can run at impressive speeds, up to 36 miles per hour (58 kilometers per hour), to chase down their target. Despite their solitary nature, leopards have occasionally been observed living in loose family groups, with mothers raising their cubs until they are old enough to fend for themselves.

o   Leopards are excellent climbers and are known for their ability to drag their prey up into trees to avoid scavengers.

o   They are the most widely distributed big cat species in the world, found in diverse habitats across Africa and parts of Asia.

o   Leopards are incredibly stealthy hunters and can approach their prey without being noticed, thanks to their spotted coat providing excellent camouflage.

o They have retractable claws, like all other big cats, which they use for climbing and catching prey.

o Leopards are powerful animals and can carry prey much larger than themselves, such as young giraffes or wildebeests.

o They are opportunistic hunters and have a varied diet that includes small to large mammals, birds, and even fish and reptiles.

o Leopards are capable of leaping horizontally up to 20 feet (6 meters) and vertically up to 10 feet (3 meters).

o Leopards are mostly solitary animals and prefer to live and hunt alone, except during mating or when a mother is raising her cubs.

o The term "leopard" is derived from the Greek word "leopardos," meaning "lion and panther."

o They are known for their distinctive, raspy call, which sounds like a saw cutting through wood and is often heard during the night.

o A leopard's spots are unique to each individual and can be used to identify and track them in the wild.

o They have a wide range of vocalizations, including growls, roars, hisses, and meows, used for communication, and establishing territory.

o Leopards have specialized whiskers, called vibrissae, that help them sense objects and navigate in the dark.

o Leopards have large nasal cavities that enhance their sense of smell, aiding them in locating prey or detecting predators.

o They are known for their agility, able to move quickly through dense vegetation and rough terrain with ease.

24. LIONS

Lions are majestic and iconic big cats belonging to the Panthera genus, which also includes tigers, leopards, and jaguars. Native to Africa, lions are known for their distinctive appearance, with tawny coats, powerful builds, and magnificent manes in males. The mane, which encircles the male's head and neck, varies in size and color, with darker manes often indicating higher testosterone levels and a dominant status within the pride.

These social cats live in groups called prides, typically consisting of related females, their cubs, and a few resident males. The lionesses work together to hunt and provide food for the pride, while the male lions protect their territory and offspring from rival males. Lions are apex predators and primarily prey on large herbivores like wildebeests, zebras, and buffalo. Their powerful jaws and sharp teeth enable them to deliver swift and deadly bites to bring down their prey.

Once widespread across much of Africa and parts of Asia, lions now face significant threats, with their populations declining due to habitat loss, human-wildlife conflict, and poaching. Conservation efforts are essential to protect these magnificent cats and preserve the intricate balance they maintain in their ecosystems as top predators. Lions remain a symbol of strength, pride, and power, earning them the nickname "king of the jungle," even though they primarily inhabit savannas and grasslands rather than dense jungles.

o   Lions are the only social big cats, living in groups called prides that can include up to 30 individuals.

o   The iconic roar of a lion can be heard from up to 5 miles (8 kilometers) away.

o   A male lion's mane serves as a sign of his maturity and dominance within the pride.

o   Lionesses are the primary hunters in the pride, working together to take down prey.

o   Lions are crepuscular animals, meaning they are most active during the early morning and late afternoon.

o   The scientific name of the lion is Panthera Leo.

o   Lions are the second-largest big cats, after tigers, with males weighing up to 550 pounds (250 kilograms).

o   Unlike other big cats, lions are highly social and often engage in playful behavior with one another.

o   Lions have specialized retractable claws, like domestic cats, that help them grip and hold onto their prey.

o   Cubs are born blind and remain vulnerable in the den for the first few weeks of life.

o   They are the national animal of several countries, including Ethiopia, Belgium, and Singapore.

o   The average lifespan of a lion in the wild is around 10 to 14 years, but they can live longer in captivity.

o   Lions can reach speeds of up to 50 miles per hour (80 kilometers per hour) in short bursts.

o   Lions have strong family bonds, and lionesses will often care for each other's cubs.

o   They are known for their communal grooming behavior, which helps strengthen social bonds within the pride.

25. MANATEES

Manatees are gentle and slow-moving marine mammals that belong to the order Sirenia. There are three species of manatees: the West Indian manatee, the Amazonian manatee, and the West African manatee. They are found in warm, shallow waters and rivers along the coasts and rivers of the Caribbean, Gulf of Mexico, and parts of South America and West Africa.

Manatees have a unique appearance, with a rounded body covered in thick, wrinkled skin and sparse hairs. They have paddle-like flippers that help them swim and navigate through the water. Their horizontally flattened tail serves as one of their primary propulsion mechanisms. Manatees are herbivores, and they primarily graze on aquatic vegetation, such as seagrasses and algae. Due to their low metabolic rate, they spend much of their time resting and conserving energy. They are capable of holding their breath for several minutes but need to surface regularly to breathe air.

Despite their large size, manatees are docile and non-aggressive creatures, earning them the nickname "sea cows." They are known for their curious and friendly behavior, often approaching boats and humans in the water. Conservation efforts are crucial to protect these unique and beloved marine mammals and ensure their survival in their natural habitats.

o   Manatees are also known as "sea cows" due to their herbivorous diet and slow, gentle nature.

o   There are three species of manatees: the West Indian manatee, the Amazonian manatee, and the West African manatee.

o   Manatees are marine mammals, but they are more closely related to elephants than to whales or dolphins.

o They have large, paddle-like flippers that they use to swim and steer through the water.

o Manatees are excellent swimmers but are generally slow-moving, cruising at about 5 miles per hour (8 kilometers per hour).

o These gentle giants can weigh up to 1,300 pounds (600 kilograms) and measure around 10 to 13 feet (3 to 4 meters) in length.

o Manatees have a low metabolic rate and spend much of their time resting and conserving energy.

o They are herbivores, primarily feeding on seagrasses, aquatic plants, and algae.

o Manatees have prehensile lips that they use to grasp and pull vegetation into their mouths.

o Unlike most other mammals, manatees have molars that continuously grow and are replaced throughout their lives.

o They can hold their breath for up to 20 minutes when resting, but they need to surface for air regularly.

o Manatees have few natural predators, but their main threats are human-related, such as boat collisions and habitat destruction.

o They are social animals and are often seen in groups or "herds," especially during the mating season.

o Manatees have a thick layer of blubber to help them regulate their body temperature in cold waters.

o Manatees are known for their curious and friendly behavior, making them popular attractions for tourists and wildlife enthusiasts.

o In some cultures, manatees were historically believed to be the mythical creatures known as "mermaids" due to their unique appearance.

26. MONKEYS

Monkeys are a diverse group of primates belonging to the suborder Haplorhini. They are characterized by their flexible hands and feet, which allow them to grasp and manipulate objects, and their forward-facing eyes that provide excellent depth perception. Monkeys are found in various habitats around the world, including tropical rainforests, savannas, and mountains.

Monkeys come in various shapes and sizes, ranging from tiny pygmy marmosets that fit in the palm of a hand to larger species like baboons and macaques. They have a wide range of behaviors and social structures. Some species, like spider monkeys and howler monkeys, are known for their exceptional agility in the trees, while others, such as macaques and vervet monkeys, are more terrestrial.

Monkeys are highly intelligent animals, and some species, like the capuchin monkey, have been observed using tools to aid in their foraging. They are also known for their complex social behaviors, living in groups that can range from a few individuals to large troops. Monkeys are herbivores, omnivores, or frugivores, depending on the species, and their diet includes fruits, leaves, insects, and sometimes small vertebrates. These charismatic and resourceful creatures continue to captivate the interest and curiosity of people around the world.

o   Monkeys belong to the order Primates, which also includes apes and humans.

o   There are over 260 known species of monkeys, ranging from tiny pygmy marmosets to larger macaques and baboons.

o   Monkeys have opposable thumbs and toes, which allow them to grip and manipulate objects with dexterity.

o   Some monkeys, like capuchin monkeys, have been observed using tools, such as using sticks to extract insects from tree bark.

o   Monkeys are highly social animals and live in various group structures, including troops, bands, and harems.

o   Many monkey species have distinct calls and vocalizations used for communication within their groups.

o   Some monkeys, like howler monkeys, have a specialized hyoid bone in their throats that amplifies their calls, making them some of the loudest animals in the world.

o   The smallest monkey in the world is the pygmy marmoset, which weighs only around 3.5 ounces (100 grams).

o   The largest monkey is the male mandrill, which can weigh up to 77 pounds (35 kilograms) and has strikingly colorful markings on its face.

o   Monkeys in the New World (the Americas) have prehensile tails, which means they can use their tails to grasp and hold onto objects, while Old World monkeys (Africa, Asia, and Europe) do not have this adaptation.

o   Some monkeys, like the squirrel monkey, have excellent leaping abilities, allowing them to move quickly and skillfully through the trees.

o   Monkey infants are called "infants" or "babies."

o   Monkeys are found in a wide range of habitats, from tropical rainforests and savannas to snowy mountains.

o   Some monkey species, like the gelada baboon, engage in "lip-flip displays" to communicate and express social status.

o   Monkeys have a well-developed sense of sight and color vision.

o   In some cultures, and mythologies, monkeys are associated with intelligence, mischief, and cleverness.

27. OCTOPUSES

Octopuses are fascinating and highly intelligent marine animals belonging to the class Cephalopoda. They are soft-bodied and have no internal or external skeleton, which allows them to squeeze through tight spaces and hide in crevices. Octopuses are found in oceans all around the world, from shallow coastal waters to the deep sea, and they are known for their remarkable abilities and behaviors.

One of the most striking features of octopuses is their eight arms, which are lined with suction cups and can regenerate if damaged. These arms are highly flexible and allow octopuses to manipulate objects with incredible precision. In addition to their arms, octopuses also have a sharp beak used for catching and eating their prey.

Octopuses are renowned for their intelligence, problem-solving abilities, and complex behaviors. They are capable of learning and have been observed using tools, recognizing patterns, and even opening jars to access food. They are also masters of camouflage, using specialized skin cells called chromatophores to change color and texture to match their surroundings, helping them avoid predators and ambush prey. Octopuses are solitary animals and have a short lifespan, typically living for only one to three years, depending on the species. These enigmatic creatures continue to captivate scientists and ocean enthusiasts, revealing more of their mysteries and captivating behaviors with each new discovery.

o   Octopuses have three hearts: two pump blood through the gills, and the third pumps it through the rest of the body.

o   They are considered the most intelligent of all invertebrates and have complex problem-solving abilities.

o   Octopuses have an incredible ability to regenerate lost limbs, including their arms.

o   Some species of octopuses, like the mimic octopus, can change both color and texture to imitate other marine creatures, such as fish and sea snakes.

o   Octopuses have a highly developed sense of touch, with thousands of specialized suction cups on their arms that allow them to taste and manipulate objects.

o   They are expert escape artists and can squeeze through small openings or use their arms to unscrew lids or open containers.

o   Octopuses have a beak made of chitin, like that of a parrot, which they use to crack open shellfish and other prey.

o   The largest species of octopus is the giant Pacific octopus, which can have a leg span of up to 16 feet (5 meters) and weigh over 100 pounds (45 kilograms).

o   Octopuses are carnivorous and primarily feed on crabs, shrimp, and fish.

o   They are solitary creatures and usually only come together to mate.

o   The common octopus has a short lifespan of about one to two years, while some deep-sea octopuses may live up to five years or more.

o   The blue-ringed octopus is one of the most venomous animals in the world, and its bite can be deadly to humans.

o   Some octopuses, like the coconut octopus, have been observed using coconut shells and other objects as portable shelters.

o   Octopuses can use jet propulsion to move quickly through the water by expelling water through a siphon.

o   The ink sac of an octopus is used as a defense mechanism to confuse predators, allowing the octopus to escape.

o   Some octopuses, like the blanket octopus, have remarkable size dimorphism, with females being much larger than males and having long, flowing "blankets" of skin used for display and defense.

28. ORANGUTANS

Orangutans are remarkable great apes belonging to the genus Pongo and are native to the rainforests of Indonesia and Malaysia. They are closely related to humans and share approximately 97% of their DNA with us, making them one of our closest living relatives. Orangutans are the largest arboreal (tree-dwelling) mammals in the world and have adapted to life in the dense canopy of tropical rainforests.

These highly intelligent and solitary primates have distinctive reddish-brown fur, which earned them the name "orangutan," meaning "person of the forest" in the Malay language. They have long, powerful arms and opposable thumbs, enabling them to swing effortlessly through the trees. Orangutans spend most of their time in the treetops, where they build sleeping nests out of leaves and branches each night.

Orangutans are frugivores, with most of their diet consisting of fruits, but they also consume leaves, bark, and insects. They have a slow reproductive rate, with females giving birth to a single offspring every six to eight years, making them particularly vulnerable to population decline.

o   Orangutans are the largest arboreal animals, spending most of their lives in trees.

o   They have an arm span of up to 8 feet (2.4 meters), which is much longer than their height.

o   Orangutans have unique throat pouches called "flanges" in adult males, which develop during adolescence.

o   They are highly intelligent and have been observed using tools, such as using sticks to extract insects or honey from tree bark.

o   Orangutans are critically endangered, with only two species remaining:

the Bornean orangutan (Pongo pygmaeus) and the Sumatran orangutan (Pongo abelii).

o   These apes have a slow reproductive rate, with females giving birth to a single offspring every six to eight years.

o   Orangutans are predominantly frugivores, with fruits making up about two-thirds of their diet.

o   Their name, "orangutan," means "person of the forest" in the Malay language.

o   Orangutans are excellent climbers and are known for their incredible agility in the treetops.

o   They build sleeping nests in trees each night, using leaves and branches.

o   Orangutans have long, shaggy hair that helps protect them from the rainforest elements.

o   Unlike other great apes, orangutans have a unique ability to close their hands tightly, giving them a powerful grip.

o   They are primarily solitary animals, with adult males being mostly solitary and females being semi-solitary.

o   Infant orangutans stay with their mothers for several years, learning essential skills for survival.

o   Orangutans have a vast vocal range, including a variety of grunts, whistles, and calls used for communication.

o   They are excellent swimmers and have been observed crossing rivers to reach new areas.

29. ORCAS

Orcas, also known as killer whales, are highly intelligent and social marine mammals belonging to the dolphin family (Delphinidae). Despite their name, they are not whales but the largest species of dolphins. Orcas are found in oceans all around the world, from the icy waters of the Arctic and Antarctic to the tropical seas. They are powerful and skilled predators, known for their cooperative hunting strategies and diverse diet, which includes fish, squid, marine mammals like seals and sea lions, and even other species of whales.

Orcas have a striking appearance with their distinctive black and white coloration, white eye patches, and sleek, streamlined bodies. They are known for their playful behavior, often leaping out of the water, riding waves, and slapping their tails on the surface. Orcas are highly social animals, living in pods that can range from a few individuals to up to 50 or more members. These pods have strong bonds, and members work together to hunt, communicate, and care for their young.

As apex predators, orcas have no natural enemies in the wild, and their intelligence and adaptability have made them highly successful in various marine environments. They are also known for their complex vocalizations and communication skills, using clicks, whistles, and calls to communicate with each other.

o   Orcas are the largest species of dolphins and are often referred to as "killer whales" due to their formidable hunting abilities, but they are not whales.

o   They have a diverse diet that includes fish, squid, marine mammals like seals and sea lions, and even other species of whales.

o   Orcas are highly intelligent and are known for their problem-solving skills and complex social behaviors.

o   They live in tightly knit, matriarchal family groups called pods, led by the oldest and most experienced female, known as the pod's matriarch.

o   Each pod has its own unique dialect of vocalizations, allowing them to communicate and maintain social bonds.

o   Orcas use echolocation, a form of sonar, to navigate, communicate, and locate prey in the water.

o   They are known for their playful behavior, often seen breaching (leaping out of the water) and spy-hopping (raising their heads out of the water to observe their surroundings).

o   Orcas have a highly developed sense of community and cooperation, working together to hunt and care for their young.

o   They are found in oceans all around the world, from the Arctic to the Antarctic, and even in tropical waters.

o   Orcas can swim at speeds of up to 34 miles per hour (56 kilometers per hour) and can travel long distances in search of food.

o   In some regions, orcas have developed unique hunting techniques, such as "wave-washing," where they create waves to knock seals off ice floes.

o   They have a diverse range of colors and patterns on their bodies, including saddle patches behind their dorsal fins, which help researchers identify individual whales.

o   Orcas are long-lived animals, with some individuals estimated to live over 70 years in the wild.

o   Some populations of orcas, known as "transient" orcas, primarily feed on marine mammals, while others, known as "resident" orcas, primarily feed on fish.

o   Orcas have been featured in various cultural stories and are symbols of power, intelligence, and community in many indigenous cultures.

30. OSTRICHES

Ostriches are fascinating flightless birds native to the savannas and deserts of Africa. They are the largest and heaviest birds in the world, with males reaching heights of up to 9 feet (2.7 meters) and weighing up to 350 pounds (160 kilograms). Ostriches have long, powerful legs that enable them to run at speeds of up to 45 miles per hour (72 kilometers per hour), making them the fastest land birds.

These large birds have unique adaptations that allow them to thrive in their arid habitats. Their long necks and keen eyesight make them excellent at spotting predators from a distance, and their powerful legs are not only for running but also for delivering powerful kicks as a defense mechanism. Ostriches are primarily herbivorous, feeding on plants, seeds, fruits, and occasionally insects and small animals.

Ostriches have distinctive plumage with predominantly black feathers on their bodies and white feathers on their wings and tail. Their wings are relatively small compared to their body size and are not used for flight. Instead, they are used for balance and courtship displays. Ostriches have unique social structures and often live in groups called flocks, led by a dominant male and female. They are known for their intriguing behaviors, such as elaborate courtship dances and communal nesting sites. Ostriches play a vital role in their ecosystems and have captured the interest of people worldwide with their remarkable physical adaptations and behaviors.

o   Ostriches are the largest and heaviest birds in the world, with males weighing up to 350 pounds (160 kilograms) and standing up to 9 feet (2.7 meters) tall.

o   Ostriches are flightless birds. Instead of flying, they use their powerful legs for running.

- o Ostriches are incredibly fast runners and can reach speeds of up to 45 miles per hour (72 kilometers per hour). They are the fastest land birds.

- o These birds have large eyes, about 2 inches (5 centimeters) in diameter, making them the largest eyes of any land animal.

- o Ostriches have excellent eyesight and can spot predators from great distances, using their height advantage.

- o They have two toes on each foot, with the inner toe having a long, sharp claw that is used for defense.

- o Their diet consists mainly of plants, including seeds, fruits, leaves, flowers, and even small insects and animals.

- o Ostriches are highly adaptable and can survive in a variety of habitats, from savannas and deserts to forests and grasslands.

- o They have a unique social structure, often living in groups called flocks, led by a dominant male and female.

- o Ostriches perform elaborate courtship displays, including dancing and feather fluffing, to attract a mate.

- o During courtship, the male ostrich will show off his vibrant black and white plumage to impress females.

- o Ostriches have communal nesting sites, where several females lay their eggs in a single nest, while the dominant female incubates them.

- o The eggs of ostriches are the largest of any bird species, measuring about 6 inches (15 centimeters) in length and weighing around 3 pounds (1.4 kilograms).

- o Ostriches are incredibly strong and have been known to defend themselves and their young against predators like lions and hyenas.

- o Ostriches have a distinctive call that sounds like a low booming or deep roar, which can be heard from a considerable distance.

31. OWLS

Owls are fascinating nocturnal birds of prey belonging to the order Strigiformes. They are found on almost every continent, except Antarctica, and have adapted to a wide range of habitats, including forests, grasslands, and deserts. Owls are renowned for their exceptional hunting abilities, with specialized adaptations that make them efficient nighttime predators.

One of the most distinctive features of owls is their forward-facing eyes, which provide excellent binocular vision and depth perception. Their eyes are large and fixed in their sockets, so owls must turn their entire heads to see in different directions, often capable of rotating up to 270 degrees. This unique ability allows them to spot and track prey without having to move their bodies.

Owls have acute hearing as well, with facial disks that help funnel sound to their ears, enabling them to pinpoint the location of prey even in complete darkness. They have silent flight, thanks to their specialized feathers that reduce turbulence and muffle noise. Their diet consists mainly of small mammals, birds, insects, and sometimes fish, depending on the species and the available prey in their habitat.

These enigmatic birds are often associated with wisdom and mystery in various cultures and folklore. Their haunting calls and nocturnal habits have sparked curiosity and admiration, making them both revered and feared creatures throughout history. With their unique adaptations and captivating behaviors, owls continue to be a subject of fascination and admiration for bird enthusiasts and wildlife observers worldwide.

o   Owls are found on every continent except Antarctica, and they have adapted to a wide range of habitats, from dense forests to open grasslands.

o Owls are nocturnal birds, meaning they are most active during the night and rest during the day.

o They have specialized feathers that allow them to fly silently, making them stealthy and efficient hunters.

o Owls have forward-facing eyes that give them excellent binocular vision, helping them judge distances accurately.

o Their eyes are so large that they cannot move within their sockets, so owls must turn their entire heads to look around, often turning up to 270 degrees.

o Owls have exceptional hearing, with some species able to detect prey through thick vegetation or snow.

o The feathers on the owl's face create a distinctive "facial disk," which helps focus sound and contributes to their excellent hearing abilities.

o Owls have powerful talons and beaks that they use to catch and eat their prey, such as mice, birds, insects, and even fish.

o Unlike most birds, owls have zygodactyl feet, with two toes facing forward and two toes facing backward, which enhances their gripping ability.

o Some owl species, like the Great Horned Owl, have tufts of feathers on their heads called "ear tufts," but these are not actually ears; their ears are located on the sides of their heads.

o The distinctive hooting sound associated with owls is made by the male during the breeding season to attract females and establish territory.

o Some owl species have specialized feather colors and patterns that help them blend into their surroundings, providing excellent camouflage.

o Owls regurgitate pellets containing indigestible parts of their prey, such as bones and fur, after they have digested the nutritious parts.

32. PANDAS

Pandas, also known as giant pandas, are beloved and iconic mammals native to the mountainous regions of central China. They are easily recognizable with their distinctive black and white markings. Pandas have a unique combination of adaptations that make them highly specialized bamboo feeders. Despite belonging to the order Carnivora, their diet consists almost exclusively of bamboo, particularly the bamboo species known as arrow bamboo.

Pandas have a stocky build, with large round heads, short tails, and strong jaws equipped to chew bamboo. Their thick woolly fur helps them withstand the cold temperatures in their mountain habitats. Pandas are primarily solitary animals and are known for their gentle demeanor. They are excellent climbers and swimmers, with the ability to navigate through bamboo forests and across streams.

Pandas have faced severe threats to their survival due to habitat loss and human encroachment. As a result, they are listed as vulnerable on the IUCN Red List of Threatened Species. Conservation efforts have been underway to protect their natural habitats and ensure the survival of these beloved and treasured animals. Pandas have captured the hearts of people worldwide, making them one of the most celebrated and protected species in the animal kingdom.

o   Pandas are primarily found in the bamboo forests of the mountains in central China.

o   Despite being classified as carnivores, pandas have evolved to be herbivores and primarily eat bamboo leaves, stems, and shoots.

o   Bamboo makes up about 99% of a panda's diet, and they can consume up to 40 pounds (18 kilograms) of bamboo each day.

o Pandas have a sixth toe, called a "pseudo thumb," that helps them manipulate bamboo and climb trees.

o The black patches around a panda's eyes are thought to help them identify each other and may act as camouflage in the shadows.

o Baby pandas are born pink and hairless, and they start developing their black and white markings after a few weeks.

o Pandas are solitary animals and are usually only found together during the breeding season or when a mother is caring for her cub.

o Giant pandas are good climbers and can also swim, although they generally prefer to stay on the ground.

o Adult pandas can weigh between 200 to 330 pounds (90 to 150 kilograms), with males typically being larger than females.

o Pandas have a specialized digestive system to process the tough fibers of bamboo, although they have the digestive system of a carnivore.

o Their scientific name is "Ailuropoda melanoleuca," which means "black and white cat-foot."

o Pandas have a "barking" vocalization that sounds like a bleating lamb.

o A panda's diet consists mainly of low-calorie bamboo, so they spend a significant portion of their day eating and resting.

o Giant pandas have a relatively slow reproductive rate, with females usually giving birth to a single cub every two to three years.

o They are considered a national treasure in China and are an important symbol of conservation efforts worldwide.

o Pandas have been a focus of extensive conservation efforts, including breeding programs in captivity and protection of their natural habitats, to help ensure their survival in the wild.

33. PEACOCKS

Peacocks are stunning and colorful birds belonging to the pheasant family, known for their extravagant and iridescent plumage. The term "peacock" technically refers to the male of the species, while the females are known as "peahens." The male peacock has a magnificent tail, or "train," consisting of elongated feathers with striking eye-spots, which they display during courtship to attract females.

These birds are native to South Asia, particularly India and Sri Lanka, but they have been introduced to various parts of the world due to their beauty and elegance. Peacocks are ground-dwelling birds, but they are skilled fliers and can take to the trees to roost at night or escape predators. They are omnivorous and feed on a variety of foods, including insects, plants, seeds, and small reptiles.

Peacocks are known for their loud and distinctive calls, especially during the breeding season, when the males put on spectacular displays to court the females. The courtship ritual involves fanning their tails, raising and lowering their wings, and emitting loud calls to attract the attention of peahens. The brilliant display of colors and patterns in a peacock's plumage has captivated humans for centuries, making them a symbol of beauty, elegance, and pride in many cultures and societies worldwide.

o   The term "peacock" technically refers to the male, while the females are called "peahens," and together, they are referred to as "peafowl."

o   The striking and colorful plumage of peacocks is an elongated tail made up of specialized feathers called "train feathers" or "coverts."

o   Peacocks are native to South Asia, particularly India and Sri Lanka.

o The vibrant colors of a peacock's plumage are not due to pigments but are the result of structural coloration, which reflects and scatters light to create the iridescent effect.

o The train feathers of a male peacock can reach up to 6 feet (1.8 meters) in length.

o Peacocks can fly despite their long and heavy tail feathers, but they typically prefer to roost in trees at night.

o They are omnivorous and feed on a variety of foods, including insects, small mammals, reptiles, plants, seeds, and even small snakes.

o Male peacocks use their extravagant display of tail feathers to attract females during courtship rituals, called "dancing."

o The courtship display involves spreading the tail feathers into a magnificent fan and vibrating them while walking in circles or facing the female.

o The peacock's call is a loud and distinctive "meow" or "pea-ock" sound, especially during the breeding season.

o Female peafowls, or peahens, are more subdued in color than males, as their plumage serves as camouflage to protect their nests.

o The collective term for a group of peafowls is a "party" or "pride."

o Peacocks can live up to 20 years in the wild, and even longer in captivity.

o The peacock is the national bird of India, where it holds cultural and religious significance.

o Peacocks are strong runners and can reach speeds of up to 10 miles per hour (16 kilometers per hour) on the ground.

o The male peacock sheds its elaborate tail feathers at the end of the breeding season, and they regrow the following year.

34. PENGUINS

Penguins are fascinating flightless birds known for their distinctive black and white plumage and their incredible adaptations for life in the water. They are found primarily in the Southern Hemisphere, with some species also inhabiting temperate regions near the equator. Penguins are highly adapted to aquatic life, with their wings evolved into flippers and their bodies streamlined for swimming.

These social and highly gregarious birds are well-known for their waddling walk on land and their remarkable swimming abilities in the water. They are excellent divers and can reach impressive depths to catch fish and other marine creatures for food. Penguins have specialized feathers that are densely packed and overlap like shingles, providing excellent insulation against the cold temperatures of their native environments.

Penguins are known for their strong sense of community and cooperation. They form large colonies where they nest, breed, and raise their chicks together. They have distinctive calls that allow them to locate their mates and chicks in crowded colonies. Penguins' unique combination of characteristics and behaviors has captured the hearts of people worldwide, making them some of the most beloved and recognizable creatures in the animal kingdom.

o   Penguins are flightless birds that evolved to be superb swimmers, with wings adapted into flippers for efficient propulsion through the water.

o   They are found mainly in the Southern Hemisphere, although some species inhabit temperate regions near the equator.

o   The Emperor Penguin is the largest penguin species, standing about 3.7 feet (1.1 meters) tall and weighing up to 88 pounds (40 kilograms).

o   The Little Blue Penguin, also known as the Fairy Penguin, is the smallest penguin species, reaching only about 16 inches (40 centimeters) in height.

o   Penguins are social animals and often form large colonies to breed, nest, and raise their chicks together.

o   They have a unique black and white plumage, which acts as camouflage when swimming, with the black back blending in with the dark depths of the ocean, and the white belly concealing them from predators below.

o   Penguins have excellent underwater vision, which helps them spot prey while swimming.

o   They are skilled divers and can reach depths of up to 1,800 feet (550 meters) to catch fish and other marine creatures.

o   Penguins can leap out of the water onto floating ice or rocky shores using their flippers to propel themselves.

o   While swimming, penguins can reach speeds of up to 15 to 25 miles per hour (24 to 40 kilometers per hour).

o   Penguins use various vocalizations, including calls, songs, and braying sounds, to communicate with each other.

o   Penguins have a specialized gland above their eyes that filters excess salt from seawater, allowing them to drink it without becoming dehydrated.

o   They have an annual molting process, during which they shed and replace their feathers. During this time, they are unable to swim and must fast until their new feathers grow in.

o   Male and female penguins often have distinct calls, which helps them locate their mates and chicks in crowded colonies.

o   Some penguin species, like the Emperor Penguin, incubate their eggs on their feet, keeping them warm with a special brood pouch.

o   Penguins are monogamous during the breeding season, and some species, like the Adélie Penguin, return to the same breeding site year after year.

35. PLATYPUSES

The platypus is one of the most fascinating and unique mammals in the world, known for its peculiar combination of features. Native to eastern Australia, the platypus is a monotreme, a group of mammals that lay eggs instead of giving birth to live young. They are the only surviving species of their family (Ornithorhynchidae) and genus (Ornithorhynchus).

The platypus has a duck-like bill, webbed feet, and a beaver-like tail, making it a semi-aquatic animal perfectly adapted for its aquatic lifestyle. Their waterproof fur keeps them warm while swimming, and they close their eyes, ears, and nostrils when underwater. The bill is filled with electroreceptors that detect electrical signals emitted by their prey, enabling them to locate food underwater, even in complete darkness.

Platypuses primarily feed on small aquatic invertebrates like insects, crustaceans, and worms. They are solitary and mostly active during the night, spending their days in burrows along riverbanks. Females lay eggs in nesting burrows and incubate them by curling their bodies around the eggs. After hatching, they nurse their young with milk secreted through mammary glands, making them one of the few mammals to produce both eggs and milk. The platypus is a treasured and iconic animal in Australia and continues to captivate the world with its extraordinary combination of features.

o   Platypuses are one of the few mammals that lay eggs, making them monotremes, a unique group of mammals.

o   The scientific name of the platypus is "Ornithorhynchus anatinus," which means "duck-like bird-snout" in Greek and Latin.

o   Platypuses are found only in eastern Australia, where they inhabit freshwater streams, rivers, and lakes.

o   They have a duck-like bill that is sensitive to touch and filled with electroreceptors, allowing them to detect electrical signals from their prey underwater.

o   The bill of a platypus is soft and pliable, making it an essential tool for finding and capturing small aquatic invertebrates.

o   Platypuses have webbed feet that help them swim, and they also use their front feet to dig burrows along riverbanks.

o   Their fur is waterproof, and they have specialized skin folds that close over their eyes, ears, and nostrils while underwater.

o   The males have venomous spurs on their hind legs. The venom is not lethal to humans but can cause severe pain and swelling.

o   Platypuses use their cheek pouches to store food while foraging, allowing them to bring food back to their burrows to eat.

o   They primarily feed on aquatic invertebrates like insects, crustaceans, and worms found in the mud and sand at the bottom of rivers and streams.

o   Platypuses are mainly nocturnal and spend much of their time underwater, where they can hold their breath for several minutes.

o   They are solitary animals and typically come together only to mate.

o   Female platypuses lay one to three eggs at a time and incubate them in a nesting burrow for about 10 days before hatching.

o   The milk produced by female platypuses contains lysozyme, an enzyme with antimicrobial properties that protect their young from infections.

o   Platypuses are excellent swimmers and can dive to depths of up to 60 feet (18 meters) while foraging for food.

o   They communicate using a range of vocalizations, including growls, grunts, and high-pitched whistles.

o   The platypus is a symbol of Australia and is featured on its 20-cent coin, reflecting its unique and cherished status in Australian culture.

36. POLAR BEARS

Polar bears are magnificent and iconic carnivorous mammals native to the Arctic regions of the Northern Hemisphere. They are the largest land carnivores and are superbly adapted to survive in the harsh, icy environments they inhabit. Polar bears have a thick layer of blubber and dense fur, which provide excellent insulation against the extreme cold temperatures.

These powerful predators are excellent swimmers and have evolved to be well-suited for a semi-aquatic lifestyle. They can swim long distances in search of food, often preying on marine mammals like seals and occasionally feeding on fish and other sources of food. Their large, powerful paws act like paddles, allowing them to swim effortlessly in icy waters.

Polar bears are solitary animals, and the only strong social bond they form is between a mother and her cubs. Females give birth to one to three cubs and care for them until they are old enough to fend for themselves. As the Arctic ice continues to shrink due to climate change, polar bears face significant challenges to their survival, making them a symbol of the urgent need for conservation efforts to protect their fragile habitats and the Arctic ecosystem.

o   Polar bears are the largest land carnivores, with adult males weighing between 900 to 1,600 pounds (410 to 725 kilograms) and standing up to 10 feet (3 meters) tall on their hind legs.

o   Their scientific name is "Ursus maritimus," which means "sea bear," reflecting their strong association with the Arctic Sea ice.

o   Polar bears have a thick layer of blubber, which can be up to 4.5 inches (11 centimeters) thick, providing insulation and buoyancy in icy waters.

o   Their fur appears white, but it is translucent, allowing sunlight to reach their black skin, which helps in retaining heat.

o Despite their size, polar bears are excellent swimmers and can cover distances of up to 60 miles (100 kilometers) at a time in search of food.

o They have a keen sense of smell, which allows them to detect prey from great distances, even beneath the ice.

o Polar bears can close their nostrils while swimming to prevent water from entering, and they can dive to depths of up to 15 feet (4.5 meters) to catch seals.

o They are primarily carnivorous, with their diet consisting mainly of seals, but they are opportunistic eaters and may also feed on fish, birds, and carrion.

o Despite being fierce predators, polar bears are also skilled at conserving energy. They can enter a state of lowered metabolic activity, known as "walking hibernation," to survive periods of food scarcity.

o Polar bears have partially webbed front paws, aiding them in swimming and acting as large paddles.

o They are excellent at conserving body heat and can withstand extremely low temperatures, withstanding temperatures as cold as -50 degrees Celsius (-58 degrees Fahrenheit).

o Polar bears have an exceptional sense of smell, capable of detecting prey from miles away, even under thick layers of ice and snow.

o They give birth to their cubs in dens made of snow and ice, where the mother provides warmth and protection until the cubs are strong enough to venture outside.

o The mothers are fiercely protective of their cubs and will defend them against potential threats, including other polar bears.

o Polar bears are known for their playful behavior, especially among young cubs, who engage in wrestling matches and sliding on the ice.

o They have specialized adaptations in their liver and kidneys to process a high-fat diet, which allows them to efficiently extract nutrients from seal blubber.

37. RABBITS

Rabbits are small mammals belonging to the family Leporidae. They are known for their long ears, powerful hind legs, and propensity to reproduce rapidly. Rabbits are found in various habitats across the world, including forests, grasslands, deserts, and even urban areas. They are highly adaptable animals and have successfully coexisted with humans in many parts of the world.

Rabbits are herbivores, meaning their diet consists of plant material like grass, leaves, and vegetables. Their digestive system is specially designed to extract maximum nutrition from the fibrous plant material they consume. Rabbits practice coprophagy, a behavior where they eat their own feces to redigest and extract more nutrients from their food.

These social animals are usually seen in groups, and they communicate with each other through various vocalizations and body language. Rabbits are well-known for their ability to reproduce quickly, with females capable of giving birth to several litters of baby rabbits, called kits, each year. To protect themselves from predators, rabbits have evolved to be fast runners and can reach speeds of up to 35 to 45 miles per hour (56 to 72 kilometers per hour) in short bursts. Their adorable appearance and gentle demeanor have made rabbits popular pets around the world, while in the wild, they play a vital role in the ecosystem as both prey and herbivores.

o   Rabbits are highly social animals and often live in groups called "colonies" or "warrens."

o   They have excellent vision and can see nearly 360 degrees without turning their heads, helping them detect potential predators.

o   Rabbits have powerful hind legs, allowing them to jump great distances and reach speeds of up to 35 to 45 miles per hour (56 to 72 kilometers per hour).

o   They are prolific breeders, with female rabbits capable of having multiple litters of babies, called kits, each year.

o   Rabbits practice coprophagy, which means they eat their own feces to redigest and extract more nutrients from their food.

o   When rabbits are happy or excited, they may jump and twist in the air, a behavior known as "binkying."

o   Rabbits have 28 teeth, including four large incisors that continuously grow throughout their lives.

o   They are crepuscular, meaning they are most active during dawn and dusk.

o   Rabbits communicate through a variety of vocalizations, including purring, growling, and honking.

o   Their ears serve multiple purposes, such as detecting sounds from long distances, regulating body temperature, and expressing emotions.

o   Domesticated rabbits can be litter-trained, making them suitable pets for indoor living.

o   Rabbits are herbivores and have a sensitive digestive system, so they need a high-fiber diet to stay healthy.

o   Rabbits have a unique courtship ritual that involves hopping around each other in a circle.

o   Contrary to popular belief, carrots are not an ideal treat for rabbits, as they are high in sugar and should be given in moderation.

o   Wild rabbits build burrows underground, called warrens, which serve as their homes and provide protection from predators and the elements.

o   Rabbits have a specialized upper lip called a "split lip" or "philtrum" that allows them to gnaw and strip the bark from trees and plants.

38. RACCOONS

Raccoons are medium-sized mammals belonging to the Procyonidae family. They are native to North America but have also been introduced to other regions around the world. Raccoons are easily recognizable by their distinctive black "mask" markings around their eyes and ringed tails. They have a compact and robust build, with sharp claws that make them excellent climbers and foragers.

Raccoons are highly adaptable and can thrive in various environments, including forests, urban areas, and wetlands. They are omnivores, meaning they have a varied diet that includes both plant matter and animals. Their diet may consist of fruits, nuts, insects, small mammals, birds, eggs, and even scavenged food from garbage cans.

These intelligent creatures are known for their problem-solving skills and dexterity, using their front paws much like hands to manipulate objects and open containers. They are mainly nocturnal and are most active during the night, using their excellent night vision and keen sense of smell to hunt for food. Raccoons are known for their curious and mischievous behavior, and while they can be considered pests in some urban areas, they play a vital role in controlling insect populations and contributing to ecosystem balance.

o   Raccoons can rotate their hind feet 180 degrees, enabling them to descend trees headfirst with ease.

o   They have a highly developed sense of touch in their front paws, which they use to explore and manipulate objects.

o   Raccoons have a diverse diet that includes fruits, nuts, insects, small mammals, birds, eggs, fish, and even human food.

o   They are skilled and adaptive foragers, capable of opening garbage cans and even complex locks to access food.

o   Raccoons are one of the few animals that can successfully wash their food before eating it, a behavior that earned them their scientific name "Procyon lotor," which means "washing bear."

o   Despite their appearance, raccoons are not related to bears; they are part of the Procyonidae family, which includes coatis and ringtails.

o   The black markings around their eyes, called "masks," may help reduce glare and improve their night vision.

o   Raccoons are mainly nocturnal but can also be active during dawn and dusk.

o   They have a unique communication system that includes a variety of vocalizations, such as chittering, growling, purring, and whining.

o   Raccoons are excellent swimmers and can dive into water to catch fish and other aquatic prey.

o   The term for a group of raccoons is called a "nursery" or a "gaze."

o   In colder regions, raccoons enter a period of inactivity during the winter called "torpor," during which their metabolic rate decreases, and they sleep for extended periods.

o   They are one of the few mammals capable of "walking" on their hind legs for short distances.

o   Raccoons have a relatively long lifespan in the wild, with some individuals living up to 5 to 7 years or more.

o   Female raccoons are dedicated mothers and usually give birth to a litter of 2 to 5 kits each spring.

39. RHINOCEROSES

Rhinoceroses, commonly known as rhinos, are large, herbivorous mammals belonging to the family Rhinocerotidae. They are among the most iconic and endangered animals in the world. Rhinos are native to Africa and Asia, with five extant species: the White Rhino, Black Rhino, Indian Rhino, Javan Rhino, and Sumatran Rhino. These magnificent creatures are easily recognized by their massive size, thick skin, and one or more horns on their snouts.

Rhinos are primarily herbivores, feeding on grasses, leaves, fruits, and other vegetation. Their size and strength make them formidable animals, and they have few natural predators in the wild. However, they have faced significant threats from poaching and habitat loss, which have led to a severe decline in their populations.

All rhino species are listed as either vulnerable, endangered, or critically endangered by the International Union for Conservation of Nature (IUCN). Conservation efforts and anti-poaching measures are critical to protecting these magnificent animals and ensuring their survival for future generations. Rhinos play a vital role in their ecosystems as grazers and seed dispersers, and their preservation is crucial for maintaining the ecological balance in their habitats.

o   Rhinoceroses are among the largest land mammals, with some species weighing up to 2 to 3 tons (1,800 to 2,700 kilograms).

o   The name "rhinoceros" comes from the Greek words "rhino" (nose) and "ceros" (horn), referring to the horn on their snouts.

o   Rhinos have thick and tough skin, which can be up to 2 inches (5 centimeters) thick, providing protection against thorny vegetation and potential predators.

o   Rhinoceroses are found in Africa and Asia, with five species remaining: White Rhino, Black Rhino, Indian Rhino, Javan Rhino, and Sumatran Rhino.

o   The White Rhino is the largest species and is named after the Dutch word "wijde" (wide), describing its broad mouth.

o   Rhinos have relatively small eyes, but their sense of smell and hearing are well-developed, aiding in detecting danger and finding food.

o   Some rhino species, like the Black Rhino, have a pointed upper lip that allows them to grasp and strip leaves from branches.

o   The horns of rhinos are made of keratin, the same material found in human fingernails and hair.

o   The horn is not attached to the skull; it grows from a mass of keratin fibers on the rhino's snout.

o   Rhinos use their horns for various purposes, including defense, establishing dominance, and digging for food.

o   Rhinos are herbivores, feeding primarily on grasses, leaves, fruits, and aquatic vegetation.

o   Rhinos are surprisingly agile and can run at speeds of up to 30 to 40 miles per hour (48 to 64 kilometers per hour) for short distances.

o   Despite their robust appearance, rhinos are known to be gentle and shy animals in their natural habitats.

o   Rhinoceroses communicate using various vocalizations, including grunts, snorts, and bellows.

o   They have a unique wallowing behavior, where they roll in mud or water to cool down, protect their skin from insects, and maintain skin moisture.

o   Rhinos are known to form strong bonds with their offspring, and some species exhibit maternal care and protection towards their young.

40. SHARKS

Sharks are a group of cartilaginous fish that have existed on Earth for more than 400 million years, making them one of the oldest and most successful vertebrate species. They are found in oceans all around the world, from shallow coastal waters to deep ocean habitats. Sharks come in various sizes, shapes, and colors, ranging from the small lanternsharks to the massive whale shark, which is the largest fish species on the planet.

Sharks are well-known for their powerful predatory nature and sharp teeth, which they use to capture and consume a wide range of prey, including fish, squid, seals, and even other sharks. Many shark species are apex predators, meaning they are at the top of the food chain and play a crucial role in maintaining the balance of marine ecosystems.

Despite their fearsome reputation, most shark species are not harmful to humans. While some sharks, such as the great white shark and tiger shark, are responsible for rare and unfortunate incidents, most shark species pose little to no threat to humans. Nevertheless, sharks face significant threats, including overfishing, bycatch, habitat destruction, and climate change, leading to the decline of shark populations. Conservation efforts are crucial to protecting these magnificent and ecologically important creatures for future generations.

o   Sharks are ancient creatures, having existed on Earth for more than 400 million years, making them older than dinosaurs.

o   There are over 500 known species of sharks, and new species are still being discovered.

o   The largest shark species is the whale shark, which can grow up to 40 feet (12 meters) long.

o   The smallest shark is the dwarf lanternshark, which measures only about 7 to 8 inches (17 to 20 centimeters) in length.

o   Sharks have a highly developed sense of smell, and some species can detect one drop of blood in a swimming pool-sized amount of water.

o   Sharks have several rows of teeth, and some species can lose and replace thousands of teeth during their lifetime.

o   Unlike most fish, sharks do not have a swim bladder to control their buoyancy. Instead, they rely on their large livers, which contain oils that make them less dense than water.

o   Some shark species, like the bull shark and river shark, are capable of surviving in both saltwater and freshwater environments.

o   Sharks have a specialized organ called the ampullae of Lorenzini, which helps them detect weak electric fields emitted by potential prey.

o   Sharks are skilled predators and have adapted to a wide range of diets, from plankton and small fish to marine mammals and other sharks.

o   Many shark species are migratory and can travel vast distances, crossing entire oceans.

o   Some sharks, like the Greenland shark, are known for their longevity and can live for several centuries.

o   Sharks play a vital role in marine ecosystems as top predators, helping to maintain the balance of marine populations and ensure healthy oceans.

o   The skin of sharks is covered in tiny tooth-like structures called dermal denticles, which reduce drag and make them more efficient swimmers.

o   Some sharks, like the hammerhead shark, have uniquely shaped heads that provide enhanced sensory capabilities and improved vision.

41. SLOTHS

Sloths are slow-moving, arboreal mammals found in the rainforests of Central and South America. They belong to the families Megalonychidae and Bradypodidae and are divided into two main groups: two-toed sloths and three-toed sloths. Despite their leisurely pace, sloths are highly adapted to their tree-dwelling lifestyle. They spend most of their time hanging upside down in trees, using their long arms and specialized claws to move and cling to branches with ease.

Sloths have a low metabolic rate and spend up to 20 hours a day sleeping or resting. Their slow movements and greenish fur often provide effective camouflage against predators like eagles and jaguars. They are herbivores, mainly feeding on leaves, flowers, and fruits found in the forest canopy. Their diet is relatively poor in nutrients, which is one reason for their slow metabolism and low energy levels.

Sloths have a unique and fascinating reproductive strategy. Female sloths give birth to a single offspring, and the mother is solely responsible for caring for the young, as sloths are solitary animals. The baby clings to its mother's fur and is carried around for several months until it can fend for itself. Although sloths face threats from habitat destruction and predation, their slow and deliberate lifestyle has allowed them to adapt to their forest homes and survive for millions of years as remarkable examples of nature's ingenuity.

o   Sloths are the slowest mammals on Earth, moving at a leisurely pace of about 0.24 miles per hour (0.4 kilometers per hour).

o   They are primarily nocturnal animals, but some species may also be active during the day.

o   Sloths are excellent swimmers and can move up to three times faster in water than on land.

o   They have a unique and symbiotic relationship with algae, which grows on their fur and helps camouflage them in the trees.

o   Sloths have a specialized adaptation in their necks that allows them to rotate their heads up to 270 degrees.

o   Some sloth species have a greenish tinge to their fur due to the algae living on them, giving them a "mossy" appearance.

o   Sloths have long claws, which can be up to 4 inches (10 centimeters) in length, helping them grip onto branches and hang upside down easily.

o   They are folivores, meaning their diet mainly consists of leaves, and their slow metabolism helps them digest the tough plant material.

o   Sloths are solitary animals, and they come together only during the mating season.

o   Female sloths give birth to a single offspring, and the baby clings to its mother's fur until it becomes independent.

o   Their fur grows from the stomach to the back, which allows rainwater to drain off easily when they hang upside down.

o   Sloths can sleep for up to 15 to 20 hours a day.

o   The two-toed sloth has two fingers on its front limbs, while the three-toed sloth has three fingers.

o   Sloths are excellent climbers and can descend from trees headfirst.

o   They have a strong grip and can often remain suspended from a branch with just one limb.

o   Sloths have a slow heartbeat, averaging around 40 to 60 beats per minute.

42. SNAKES

Snakes are elongated, legless reptiles belonging to the suborder Serpentes. They are found on every continent except Antarctica and have adapted to a wide range of habitats, including forests, deserts, grasslands, and aquatic environments. Snakes are well-known for their ability to swallow their prey whole, thanks to their highly flexible jaws and lack of limbs. Their bodies are covered in scales, and they move by slithering, using their muscular belly scales to push against the ground.

Snakes are carnivorous predators, with a diet that typically includes insects, rodents, birds, and other small animals. Some larger snake species can consume larger prey, such as deer and even other snakes. They possess specialized heat-sensing organs called pit organs, located between their eyes and nostrils, which allow them to detect the body heat of their prey accurately.

Snakes play vital roles in ecosystems by controlling populations of prey species and serving as both predator and prey. While some snakes are venomous and pose a threat to humans, most snake species are harmless and help maintain ecological balance. Snakes are fascinating creatures, often shrouded in mythology and symbolism across various cultures, representing both fear and respect for their incredible adaptations and secretive nature.

o   Snakes have no eyelids. Instead, they have transparent scales covering their eyes, known as spectacle or brille, which are shed along with the rest of their skin.

o   Some snake species can go for several months without eating, depending on factors like their size, habitat, and metabolism.

o   Snakes are excellent escape artists and can fit through narrow openings due to their flexible bodies and lack of limbs.

o   The world's smallest snake is the Barbados threadsnake, which can be as tiny as 4 inches (10 centimeters) long.

o   The largest snake species, the green anaconda, can grow up to 29 feet (8.8 meters) in length and weigh over 500 pounds (227 kilograms).

o   Some snakes can "fly" through the air by gliding from tree branches, using their body as a makeshift parachute.

o   Snakes have a unique ability to sense vibrations in the ground, helping them detect approaching predators or prey.

o   Snake venom is not always used to kill prey; some snakes use it primarily for defense, to deter predators or threats.

o   Snakes shed their skin periodically as they grow. The process, called ecdysis, helps them remove old or damaged skin.

o   Some snakes, like the king cobra, possess venom strong enough to kill an adult elephant.

o   Snakes have a specialized sense organ called Jacobson's organ, which enables them to detect and analyze scents.

o   There are around 3,000 known species of snakes, with new ones still being discovered by scientists.

o   The python family of snakes can go for weeks or months without eating after consuming a large meal.

o   Snakes rely on their forked tongues to "taste" the air and pick up scent molecules, helping them locate prey or potential mates.

o   Some snake species, like the blind snake, are completely harmless and have no venom or fangs.

o   The sidewinding motion is a unique way some desert-dwelling snakes move, using a sideways slithering motion to traverse the sand.

43. SNOW LEOPARDS

Snow leopards (Panthera uncia) are elusive and magnificent big cats native to the mountainous regions of Central and South Asia. They are well-adapted to life in harsh, cold environments, inhabiting high-altitude areas ranging from 9,800 to 17,000 feet (3,000 to 5,500 meters) above sea level. Snow leopards are renowned for their stunning beauty, with thick, pale gray fur adorned with black rosettes and spots, providing excellent camouflage in their rocky habitats.

These solitary and elusive predators are highly skilled climbers, able to traverse steep and rugged terrains with ease. Their long, powerful tails help maintain balance and act as a warm covering when curled around their bodies during rest. Snow leopards have keen eyesight, allowing them to spot potential prey from great distances. They primarily feed on wild sheep and goats, as well as smaller mammals like marmots and hares.

Snow leopards are listed as vulnerable by the International Union for Conservation of Nature (IUCN) due to the threats they face, including habitat loss, poaching, and retaliatory killings by local communities to protect their livestock. Conservation efforts are essential to safeguard these majestic creatures and preserve the fragile mountain ecosystems they call home. The conservation of snow leopards not only protects a critically endangered species but also helps maintain the balance of the unique environments in which they thrive.

o   Snow leopards are well-adapted to the cold, with a thick fur coat that insulates them from harsh mountain temperatures.

o   Their long and bushy tails, which are about as long as their bodies, act as a balance aid and help them navigate rocky terrain.

o   Snow leopards are the only big cats with solid, smoky-gray or pale greenish eyes. Their eyes have a unique structure that allows them to see well in low light.

o   They are excellent climbers and can leap distances of up to 50 feet (15 meters) in a single bound.

o   Snow leopards have large, powerful paws that help distribute their weight evenly on snow and protect them from sinking.

o   Despite their agility, snow leopards are rarely seen in the wild due to their elusive nature and remote habitats.

o   The snow leopard's vocalizations include growls, hisses, and chuffing sounds, but they are generally silent predators.

o   Their preferred prey includes wild sheep, goats, and smaller mammals such as marmots and hares.

o   Snow leopards are solitary animals, except during the mating season and when a female has cubs.

o   Female snow leopards give birth to two or three cubs, usually in a hidden den made in rocky crevices or caves.

o   They have a unique hunting technique, known as "stalk and ambush," where they patiently wait for hours to get close to their prey before pouncing.

o   Snow leopards are incredibly elusive, and their population estimates are challenging to determine accurately.

o   In cold climates, snow leopards can conserve energy by reducing their metabolic rate, allowing them to survive on limited food.

o   Snow leopards have distinct facial markings, and no two individuals have the same pattern of rosettes and spots.

o   Conservation efforts are vital to protect snow leopards, as they are classified as vulnerable, with an estimated 4,000 to 6,500 individuals remaining in the wild.

44. SQUIRRELS

Squirrels are small to medium-sized rodents belonging to the Sciuridae family. They are found all over the world, except in Australia and Antarctica. Squirrels have adapted to various environments, including forests, woodlands, urban areas, and even deserts. These agile and quick creatures are easily recognizable by their bushy tails, which they use for balance, communication, and warmth.

Squirrels are known for their impressive climbing and jumping abilities, thanks to their powerful hind legs and sharp claws. They are primarily herbivores, feeding on a diet that includes nuts, seeds, fruits, and occasionally insects or bird eggs. Squirrels are known for their hoarding behavior, storing excess food in various caches to retrieve during times of scarcity, which contributes to the spread of tree seeds and helps maintain forest ecosystems.

Squirrels play a vital role in many ecosystems as seed dispersers, helping to plant trees and propagate plant species. They are essential members of the food chain, serving as prey for numerous predators, including birds of prey, snakes, and mammals like foxes and cats. These adaptable and resourceful creatures have become a familiar and endearing part of many landscapes, adding charm and liveliness to the natural world and our neighborhoods.

o   Squirrels have four front teeth that never stop growing, and they continuously wear them down by gnawing on objects like nuts and branches.

o   Some species of squirrels can jump more than 10 times their body length in a single leap.

o   Squirrels have excellent eyesight, with a wide field of vision that helps them detect potential predators.

o   Squirrels have a special adaptation called "zigras maneuver," where they flick their tails and use specific calls to deceive potential predators.

o   They are known for their caching behavior, burying nuts and seeds in the ground for later use. However, they often forget where they buried some of their caches, inadvertently helping to plant new trees.

o   Squirrels have a unique way of handling acorns, rotating them and using their sharp claws to remove the caps quickly.

o   Some species of squirrels, like flying squirrels, are capable of gliding through the air using a flap of skin between their front and hind legs.

o   The word "squirrel" comes from the Greek word "skiouros," which means "shadow-tailed."

o   Squirrels are incredibly nimble climbers, able to descend a tree headfirst by rotating their hind feet 180 degrees.

o   Some squirrels, like the Arctic ground squirrel, hibernate during the winter, dropping their body temperature and metabolism to conserve energy.

o   Squirrels are excellent swimmers and can use their bushy tails as rudders while in the water.

o   The eastern gray squirrel has a distinctive mating behavior called the "mating chase," where multiple males pursue a female in a playful and acrobatic manner.

o   Squirrels have a highly developed sense of smell, which helps them locate food and detect danger.

o   They have a diverse diet, including nuts, seeds, fruits, fungi, insects, and even bird eggs.

o   Squirrels can learn and remember complex spatial information, such as the location of their food caches.

o   There are more than 200 species of squirrels, ranging from tiny African pygmy squirrels to large tree squirrels like the Malabar giant squirrel.

45. STINGRAYS

Stingrays are a group of flat-bodied, cartilaginous fish belonging to the family Dasyatidae. They are found in various marine environments, ranging from shallow coastal waters to the open ocean. Stingrays are known for their distinctive flattened body shape, with wide pectoral fins resembling wings. These fins enable them to glide gracefully through the water, giving them a distinctive appearance as they "fly" underwater.

Stingrays possess a long, whip-like tail, which often has one or more venomous barbs near the base. These barbs can cause painful stings if a stingray feels threatened and uses its tail in defense. However, stingrays are generally not aggressive and prefer to avoid human interactions. They have a keen sense of smell and electroreceptors on their skin, allowing them to detect prey hidden in the sand.

Stingrays are carnivorous and primarily feed on small fish, crustaceans, and mollusks. They are valuable members of marine ecosystems, contributing to the control of prey populations and playing a role in nutrient cycling. While some stingray species are endangered or vulnerable due to overfishing and habitat degradation, many others thrive in their natural environments, making them an essential part of the marine biodiversity we must protect and conserve.

o   Stingrays are closely related to sharks and belong to the same class of fish, Chondrichthyes.

o   There are more than 200 species of stingrays, ranging in size from a few inches to several feet across.

o   The giant freshwater stingray, found in Southeast Asia, is the largest species and can grow up to 16.5 feet (5 meters) in width.

o   Stingrays are named after their unique barbed stingers, called spines, located on the base of their tails. These stingers can deliver venom to predators or threats.

o   Stingrays have a venomous mucus coating on their skin, which acts as a defense mechanism against potential predators.

o   Despite their venomous stingers, stingrays are generally docile and prefer to avoid confrontations with humans.

o   They have specialized sensing organs called ampullae of Lorenzini, which help them detect electrical signals produced by prey buried in the sand.

o   Stingrays are excellent at camouflaging themselves in their sandy or muddy habitats, making them challenging to spot.

o   Some species of stingrays, like the spotted eagle ray, are known for their acrobatic leaps out of the water, a behavior known as "breaching."

o   Stingrays give birth to live young, with the female carrying the developing embryos in her body until they are ready to be born.

o   Some species of stingrays, like the manta ray, are filter feeders, using their gill rakers to strain plankton and small organisms from the water.

o   Stingrays have a remarkable ability to regenerate lost or damaged fins, including their stingers.

o   They are social animals and can be found in groups called "fevers" or "schools."

o   Stingrays have a unique way of feeding called "crushing." They use their flat teeth to grind the shells of mollusks and crustaceans.

o   Stingrays are relatively long-lived animals, with some species living up to 20 years or more in the wild.

46. TIGERS

Tigers (Panthera tigris) are majestic big cats and one of the most iconic and recognizable animals in the world. They are native to various parts of Asia, including India, Russia, and Southeast Asian countries. Tigers are well-known for their striking orange coats with black stripes, which serve as effective camouflage in their forest habitats.

Tigers are powerful and agile predators, capable of taking down large prey such as deer, wild boars, and even young elephants. They are solitary animals, with adult males typically maintaining territories that encompass the territories of several females. Tigers are excellent swimmers and often bathe in water bodies to cool off and escape the heat.

Despite their fearsome reputation, tigers are under threat due to habitat loss, poaching, and conflicts with humans. Several tiger subspecies are endangered, and conservation efforts are critical to ensuring their survival in the wild. Tigers hold a significant cultural and symbolic value, being revered and feared in various societies and religions, making their conservation efforts crucial not only for their survival as a species but also for preserving the cultural heritage tied to these magnificent creatures.

o   Tigers are the largest cat species in the world, with some males weighing over 660 pounds (300 kilograms).

o   Their iconic coat with black stripes is unique to each individual, similar to a human fingerprint.

o   Tigers have excellent night vision, enabling them to hunt effectively in low-light conditions.

o   Tigers have retractable claws, allowing them to keep their sharp claws hidden when not in use.

o   A tiger's roar can be heard up to 2 miles (3.2 kilometers) away and is one of the loudest sounds produced by any land animal.

o   Tigers are solitary animals, and their territories can range from 10 to 100 square miles (25 to 260 square kilometers).

o   They have a high success rate in hunting, with a success rate of about 20-25% in catching their prey.

o   Tigers are excellent jumpers and can leap up to 33 feet (10 meters) in a single bound.

o   There are six surviving subspecies of tigers: Bengal, Indochinese, Malayan, Siberian, South China, and Sumatran.

o   The Siberian tiger, also known as the Amur tiger, is the largest and heaviest subspecies, found in the Russian Far East.

o   Tigers are mostly solitary, but they communicate with each other using vocalizations, body language, and scent markings.

o   Tigers have a unique way of killing their prey by using their powerful bite to crush the neck or suffocate the victim.

o   Despite being powerful predators, tigers are excellent climbers and can climb trees to rest or escape danger.

o   A tiger's stripes are not only on their fur but also on their skin, making them truly unique.

o   The white tiger is a rare color variation caused by a genetic mutation, and they are not a separate subspecies.

o   Tigers have been the subject of myths, legends, and religious beliefs in various cultures throughout history, making them both admired and feared animals.

47. TURTLES

Turtles are reptiles belonging to the order Testudines. They are characterized by their hard, bony shells, which provide excellent protection and serve as their distinctive feature. Turtles have been around for millions of years and have adapted to various environments, including oceans, rivers, lakes, and terrestrial habitats. Their evolutionary success can be attributed to their unique shell, which provides both defense against predators and support for their bodies.

Turtles have a diverse diet, with different species being herbivorous, omnivorous, or carnivorous. Some turtles are adapted to a fully aquatic lifestyle, such as sea turtles, while others, like tortoises, are primarily terrestrial. Turtles have a slow metabolism, which allows them to survive for long periods without food and endure harsh conditions.

Turtles are known for their longevity, with some species living well over a century. They are also famous for their migratory behavior, with sea turtles traveling vast distances between their nesting and feeding grounds. Despite their slow movement on land, turtles are agile swimmers in the water, using their webbed feet to propel themselves with grace and efficiency. Their existence on Earth has witnessed many changes, and their presence serves as a reminder of the incredible diversity of life and the importance of conservation efforts to protect these ancient and captivating creatures.

o   Turtles are one of the oldest reptile groups, dating back more than 220 million years, even before dinosaurs appeared.

o   The largest species of turtle is the leatherback sea turtle, which can weigh up to 2,000 pounds (900 kilograms) and measure over 7 feet (2.2 meters) in length.

o   The shell of a turtle is made up of around 50 different bones, including the ribs, spine, and breastbone, all fused together to form a protective structure.

o   Turtles are ectothermic, meaning they rely on external sources of heat to regulate their body temperature.

o   Some turtles, like the box turtle, can completely retract their head and limbs into their shell for protection.

o   The sex of some turtle species is determined by the incubation temperature during their development. Warmer temperatures produce more females, while cooler temperatures result in more males.

o   Sea turtles can navigate long distances during their annual migrations, sometimes crossing entire oceans to reach their nesting or feeding grounds.

o   The upper part of a turtle's shell is called the carapace, and the lower part is called the plastron.

o   Turtles have a slow growth rate, with some species taking several decades to reach their full size.

o   The oldest recorded turtle lived to be 188 years old, making them one of the longest-living animals on Earth.

o   Some species of turtles are capable of hibernating in cold climates to survive the winter months.

o   Turtles have excellent eyesight both in and out of water, and they can see color.

o   The alligator snapping turtle has a unique hunting method: it uses its tongue to lure fish into its mouth by wiggling it like a worm.

o   Turtles have a sharp beak instead of teeth, which they use to bite and tear their food.

o   Turtles have unique ways of breathing; some can breathe through their cloaca, while others have specialized adaptations to extract oxygen from water through gills.

48. WHALES

Whales are large marine mammals belonging to the order Cetacea. They are divided into two main suborders: baleen whales (Mysticeti) and toothed whales (Odontoceti). Whales are known for their immense size, intelligence, and strong sense of social structure. They are found in oceans worldwide, from polar regions to tropical waters, and their migration patterns can cover thousands of miles each year.

Baleen whales are filter feeders, using baleen plates in their mouths to trap small organisms, such as krill and plankton, from the water. Toothed whales, on the other hand, have specialized teeth and primarily feed on fish, squid, and other marine creatures. Whales communicate using a variety of vocalizations, including songs, clicks, and whistles, which are essential for social interaction and echolocation.

Whales are some of the most intelligent and social animals in the world. They live in family groups, known as pods, and display complex behaviors such as hunting cooperatively, caring for their young, and playing. These magnificent creatures have captured the fascination of humans for centuries and are now a focus of conservation efforts to protect their fragile marine habitats and ensure their survival for future generations.

o   Whales are the largest animals on Earth, with the blue whale being the largest known species, reaching lengths of up to 100 feet (30 meters) and weighing as much as 200 tons.

o   Whales are mammals, which means they give birth to live young and nurse their babies with milk.

o   Blue whales have hearts that can weigh as much as a car and are large enough for a human to swim through their major blood vessels.

o   The humpback whale is known for its intricate and beautiful songs, which can last for up to 20 minutes and be heard over long distances.

o   Whales are incredibly social creatures and often travel in pods, with some pods consisting of hundreds of individuals.

o   Whales communicate using a combination of vocalizations, body language, and echolocation.

o   Some species of whales, like the gray whale, undertake long migrations covering thousands of miles each year.

o   The sperm whale is the deepest diving mammal, capable of descending to depths of up to 7,380 feet (2,250 meters) in search of food.

o   Whales play a vital role in marine ecosystems by regulating food chains and carbon sequestration, helping to combat climate change.

o   Many whale species have baleen plates in their mouths, which they use to filter tiny organisms like krill and plankton from the water.

o   The narwhal, a type of toothed whale, is famous for its long, spiral-shaped tusk, which is actually a specialized tooth.

o   Whales have a layer of blubber under their skin that helps them stay warm in cold water and acts as an energy reserve during long migrations.

o   Whales can breach (jump out of the water) and spyhop (raise their heads vertically out of the water) for various reasons, including communication and orientation.

o   The blue whale's tongue alone can weigh as much as an elephant, and it can consume up to 4 tons of krill per day.

o   The gray whale is known for its friendly and curious behavior, often approaching boats and interacting with humans.

o   Whales have been the subject of many myths, legends, and stories across cultures throughout history, contributing to their symbolic importance and cultural significance.

49. WOLVES

Wolves (Canis lupus) are highly social and intelligent carnivores belonging to the Canidae family. They are native to various parts of the Northern Hemisphere, including North America, Europe, and Asia. Wolves have a distinctive appearance with a powerful body, sharp teeth, keen senses, and a bushy tail. They are well-adapted to various habitats, including forests, grasslands, tundra, and mountains.

Wolves are known for their strong pack mentality, living and hunting in cooperative family groups called packs. These packs are essential for their survival, enabling them to take down large prey and defend their territory from potential threats. Each pack has a well-defined hierarchy, with an alpha pair leading the group.

Wolves are opportunistic predators, primarily feeding on ungulates like deer, elk, and moose, but they can also eat smaller mammals and birds. Their howling is a significant means of communication, used for territorial defense, calling pack members, and coordinating hunts. Wolves are an integral part of many ecosystems, and conservation efforts are crucial to ensure their long-term survival and maintain the ecological balance in their natural habitats.

o   Wolves are highly intelligent animals, with problem-solving abilities similar to domestic dogs.

o   They have an exceptional sense of smell, capable of detecting scents from miles away.

o   Wolves have specialized vocalizations, including howls, growls, barks, and whines, to communicate with each other.

o   A wolf's howl can be heard over several miles and serves as a means of long-distance communication between pack members.

o   Wolves are social animals that live in close-knit family units called packs, typically consisting of an alpha male and female, their offspring, and other subordinate members.

o   The alpha pair leads the pack, making critical decisions about hunting and protecting the territory.

o   Wolves are cooperative hunters, often working together to take down large prey, which can include animals much larger than themselves.

o   They are opportunistic feeders and can eat a wide variety of animals, including deer, elk, moose, small mammals, birds, and even fish.

o   Wolves have a well-developed system of body language and facial expressions for communicating with pack members.

o   The gestation period for a female wolf is about 63 days, and she typically gives birth to a litter of 4 to 6 pups.

o   Wolf pups are born blind and deaf and rely on their parents and older siblings for care and protection.

o   Wolves play an essential role in maintaining ecosystem balance by controlling prey populations and preventing overgrazing by herbivores.

o   They are excellent runners, capable of reaching speeds of up to 35 miles per hour (56 kilometers per hour).

o   Wolves are monogamous animals, and mated pairs often stay together for life.

o   Gray wolves, also known as timber wolves, are the most widespread wolf species and can be found in North America, Europe, and Asia.

o   Wolves have a strong sense of loyalty to their pack, and they will defend and protect each other, even risking their lives for the good of the group.

o   The return of wolves to certain ecosystems has led to positive effects, known as "trophic cascades," where their presence positively impacts plant and animal populations down the food chain.

50. ZEBRAS

Zebras are herbivorous mammals belonging to the Equidae family, which also includes horses and donkeys. They are native to Africa and are best known for their distinctive black and white stripes, which serve as a form of camouflage and protection against predators. Zebras have a unique pattern of stripes that varies among species and individuals, making each zebra's coat pattern as unique as a human fingerprint.

Zebras are highly social animals that live in family groups called herds. Within the herd, there is a dominant male known as the stallion, leading a group of females and their offspring. Zebras have excellent hearing and eyesight, allowing them to detect predators from a distance. When threatened, they can run at high speeds, reaching up to 40 miles per hour (64 kilometers per hour) to escape danger.

Zebras primarily graze on grasses, and their digestive system is well-adapted to break down tough vegetation. The stripes on a zebra's coat are not only for camouflage but also play a role in social communication within the herd. Zebra herds often form temporary associations with other herbivores like wildebeests and antelopes, creating mixed-species groups that provide mutual protection against predators. These unique and captivating animals are an integral part of the African savannas, contributing to the diversity and beauty of the wildlife in their natural habitats.

o   Zebras have a unique black and white striped coat, and each individual's pattern is distinct, much like a human fingerprint.

o   There are three main species of zebras: the plains zebra, the Grevy's zebra, and the mountain zebra.

o   The Grevy's zebra is the largest and most endangered of the three species, found primarily in parts of East Africa.

o   Zebras are excellent runners and can reach speeds of up to 40 miles per hour (64 kilometers per hour) to escape predators.

o   When a zebra is born, its stripes are brown and become black as it matures.

o   The stripes on a zebra's coat are thought to serve as camouflage, making it difficult for predators to single out an individual in a running herd.

o   Zebras are social animals and live in family groups known as herds, usually consisting of a dominant male (stallion) and several females.

o   Zebras have a strong sense of smell and hearing, which helps them detect predators like lions and hyenas.

o   Despite their resemblance to horses, zebras are not easily domesticated and are generally wild animals.

o   The sounds zebras make include barks, snorts, and whinnying, and they use vocalizations to communicate with each other.

o   Zebras have a mutualistic relationship with certain bird species called oxpeckers, which pick ticks and parasites from the zebra's skin.

o   When a group of zebras stands together, their collective black and white stripes create an optical illusion known as "dazzle camouflage," making it difficult for predators to determine an individual's size and direction of movement.

o   The mountain zebra has a dewlap (a flap of skin) on its throat, which distinguishes it from other zebra species.

o   Zebras are non-territorial animals and will often share grazing areas with other herbivores, forming mixed-species groups for added protection against predators.

o   The pattern and spacing of zebras' stripes are unique to each individual, which researchers have used to identify and track zebras in the wild.

o   Zebras are found in various habitats, including grasslands, savannas, and mountainous regions, across several African countries.

MENTAL BOMB
Our goal is to entertain and to blow your mind!

Visit us online at MentalBomb.com
Home for the best illusions, riddles, games, and fun facts!

Follow

Facebook: Mental-Bomb-
Instagram: mental_bomb_
Pinterest: Mental_Bomb
Twitter: MentalBomb_